The Theology of
William Porcher DuBose

To Don
with thanks
RBS

The Theology of
William Porcher DuBose

Life, Movement, and Being

ROBERT BOAK SLOCUM

University of South Carolina Press

© 2000 University of South Carolina

Published in Columbia, South Carolina, by the
University of South Carolina Press

04   03   02   01   00   5   4   3   2   1

Library of Congress Cataloging-in-Publication Data

Slocum, Robert Boak, 1952–
    The theology of William Porcher Dubose : life, movement, and being /
Robert Boak Slocum.
        p. cm.
    Includes bibliographical references and index.
    ISBN 1-57003-347-1 (alk. paper)
    1. Dubose, William Porcher, 1836–1918.   I. Title.
BX5995.D8 S57   2000
230'.3'092—dc21   00-008236

*Frontispiece: William Porcher DuBose, courtesy of the Archive, The University of the
South, Sewanee, Tennessee*

Contents

Preface

William Porcher DuBose is recognized and appreciated by many as the most original and creative theologian to appear in the more than 200-year history of the Episcopal Church. He published seven books of theological importance, including an autobiographical work, and various theological articles. DuBose's life is commemorated as a "lesser feast" of *The Episcopal Calendar of the Church Year* on August 18.

Unfortunately, DuBose's work is much more widely honored than understood or applied to the questions facing theologians and members of the church today. Two collections of selected excerpts of DuBose's writings appeared in the 1980s. These anthologies include introductory materials that lament the relative "oblivion," "neglect," and "limited" influence of DuBose's theological contribution.

DuBose uses a "spiral" style of writing that can be difficult to follow. Although his writing is convoluted and at times may seem repetitive, DuBose's use of language brings a dynamic and open-ended dimension to his work. His theology is not confined by static forms of expression. He subtly develops and weaves together his various themes as he considers and reconsiders the points of his study. DuBose cannot readily be categorized or labeled, and he left no distinctive "school" of thought. Nevertheless, his work has a significant contribution to make to theology and the life of the church today.

For DuBose, theology is deeply connected with the experience of the Christian life as lived—especially in the context of the life of the church. His theology is based in and verified by the truth known through experience. For DuBose, a real theology of salvation must really *save*.

DuBose's system of theology is a theology of salvation which culminates in his theology of the church. Christ is made present for our salvation by the Spirit through the church. Pneumatology is a point of synthesis in DuBose's work. His ecclesiology is preeminently an ecumenical theology, as the unity of the church is the work of the Spirit. DuBose emphasizes the unity we can discover and share with each other in Christ for salvation.

This study presents a biographical study of DuBose that draws out the parallels between key experiences in his life and major themes in his published theology. It presents a consideration of the role of experience in his theological method, and an analysis of his theological system in terms of his soteriology, christology, pneumatology, and ecclesiology. It also explores the relevance of DuBose's theological vision for the life and unity of the church today.

Acknowledgments

This work reflects the help and support of many. I want to acknowledge all my teachers at the Marquette University Department of Theology, including D. Thomas Hughson, S.J., the director of the study that was the basis for this book; Patrick Carey; Richard A. Edwards; Bradford E. Hinze; Philip J. Rossi, S.J.; George H. Tavard, A.A.; and Wanda Zemler-Cizewski. Each has contributed in ways that are reflected in this book.

I also want to acknowledge those teachers in my earlier programs of study who were especially formative and helpful for my theological studies, including Reginald H. Fuller of the Virginia Theological Seminary and, from time to time, the School of Theology of the University of the South and Nashotah House Seminary; James E. Griffiss of Nashotah House Seminary and more recently Seabury-Western Seminary; and Don S. Armentrout of the School of Theology of the University of the South. I am also reminded of a visit with Girault M. Jones at his residence "Meanwhile" in Sewanee when the former bishop of Louisiana and chancellor of the University of the South suggested that I take up the study of DuBose. I also want to thank William H. Barnwell, who was serving as Associate Rector at Trinity Church, New Orleans, when he suggested that I draw out the meaning of DuBose's theology of atonement.

I particularly appreciate those librarians who have gone out of their way to help me in my research work, including Annie Armour-Jones, James W. Dunkly, and John L. Janeway IV, of the University of the South; and Michael Tolan, Anne Brosowsky, Leigh Ann Barnett, and Christi Hart of Nashotah House Seminary.

Another version of the first chapter of this study appeared as "The Lessons of Experience and the Theology of William Porcher DuBose" in the *Anglican Theological Review*, and portions of that article are reprinted with permission.

Special thanks also go to Barry Blose, acquisitions editor of the University of South Carolina Press, who challenged and encouraged me to turn an earlier text into this book. I also thank my wife, Sheryl Slocum, of Alverno College, who helped me with grace and firmness to make the editorial changes that were needed. The index was prepared by Elizabeth Anderson, who also assisted by proofreading the manuscript.

I am dedicating this work to a Lutheran pastor, Don S. Armentrout, and a Jesuit priest, D. Thomas Hughson, S.J., who have taught me much. I pray that all our work may be to the greater glory of God, and the fulfilling of Jesus' prayer that we may all be one.

I also dedicate this work to my family and household—my wife, Sheryl; our children, Claire Marie, Rebecca, and Jacob; and our friend Helen Depew. They have shared with me the challenges and sacrifices of this work, and taught me much about love.

CHAPTER 1

The Lessons of Experience

DuBose's Life and Work

William Porcher DuBose (April 11, 1836–August 18, 1918) is appreciated for the depth, originality, and beauty of the theological contribution that he made. His work earned him a place of distinction in the Episcopal Church and recognition outside his church. He was described by a commentator in 1908 as "one of the foremost philosophical theologians of our time." In 1912, a reviewer characterized him as "a writer of striking originality and fine insight, who has set himself the task of reconciling theology with modern ideas." Certainly, he was one who thought for himself. Along with other writings, DuBose published seven books of theological importance. Although DuBose's theological writings concerned the Scriptures, they were not biblical commentaries as such. DuBose explains in *The Reason of Life* that he seeks to give the "epexegesis" rather than the "exegesis," thus providing "not just what the Apostle says or wishes to say or even means to say by what he says, but what I believe to be the postulates or presuppositions of what he says."[1] Long after his death, he was described in 1985 as "one of the very truly *systematic* theologians Anglicanism has produced anywhere, and certainly one of the best."[2] *The Episcopal Calendar of the Church Year* commemorates his life as a lesser feast on August 18.

What went into the making of so great a mind and man? What is distinctive about his way of doing theology that leads people to call him "original," "creative," and "striking"? For DuBose, theology was not merely an intellectual pursuit; instead, theology was deeply rooted in human experience. In fact, his theology was formed through his own life experiences, and he believed any theological argument should be tested in light of others' experiences. For DuBose, true theology would ring true to the experiences of real life, making sense of those experiences and proving itself sensible in light of them.

William Porcher DuBose's ancestors were Norman French Huguenots who settled in South Carolina in 1686. His family was made up of planters.[3] He was born on April 11, 1836, in Winnsboro, about thirty miles north of Columbia. His family owned a large plantation of about 2,500 acres, known as "Farmington," in Fairfield County, in the Up-Country of South Carolina. When DuBose was eight years old they moved to another plantation, "Roseland." It was about seven miles closer than "Farmington" to Winnsboro, where Mt. Zion College was available for the education of DuBose and his brother.[4] His father, Theodore Samuel Marion DuBose, was serious about education and learning. His library included the classics of poetry and prose, which his family often read aloud at family gatherings in the evening.[5]

DuBose did well in his early schooling, but he struggled with mathematics. This led his father to send him to the South Carolina Military College, The Citadel, in Charleston, before he went to the University of Virginia. DuBose was a very successful cadet at The Citadel. He graduated with first honors in December 1855. He also served as the ranking officer in his class, and as an assistant professor in the English department. He later studied Latin, Greek, French, and moral science at the University of Virginia, and earned the Master of Arts degree in 1859. At the University of Virginia, he studied under Dr. Basil Gildersleeve, a noted scholar of Greek in his day. In October 1859, DuBose entered the diocesan seminary in Camden, South Carolina.

DuBose was called away from seminary by the Civil War in his middle or second year in 1861. At first he served as an adjutant. During the Civil War he was wounded three times, including two wounds at the Second Battle of Manassas (Second Bull Run) in Virginia on August 30, 1862. He was later taken a prisoner of war and nearly killed after he encountered a bivouac of enemy soldiers on a reconnaissance mission at Boonesboro Gap in Maryland, after he was almost shot by one of the soldiers who captured him.[6] He was held as a prisoner of war at Fort Delaware, where he came to be infested with lice. Some time after being returned to his Army in an exchange of prisoners, influential friends in the church and the government arranged for DuBose to be ordained and commissioned as a chaplain in the Confederate Army.[7] On December 13, 1863, DuBose was ordained deacon. Earlier that year, while on furlough from the army, he married Anne ("Nannie") Barnwell Peronneau of

Charleston, after a two-year engagement. He served as a chaplain in the army until the end of the war. He held the rank of captain.[8]

After the war, in October 1865, DuBose became rector of St. John's, Fairfield County, which included St. John's, Winnsboro, and St. Stephen's, Ridgeway.[9] He was ordained priest on September 9, 1866. His first daughter, Susie, was born on October 15, 1866. His rectory was in Winnsboro at this time, and he taught Greek at Mount Zion College in Winnsboro. He became rector of Trinity Church, Abbeville, on January 1, 1868. His second daughter, May, was born on that same day. On May 15, 1870, his first son, William Haskell, was born. In 1870, the Bishop of South Carolina asked for an assistant bishop. The election for this episcopal office took place at the 1871 diocesan convention. DuBose became a serious candidate during the course of the convention, and narrowly missed election. He termed this "one of the most fortunate escapes of my life."[10]

In 1871, DuBose was called to the University of the South at Sewanee, Tennessee, as chaplain of the university and professor of moral science. He began his "life task" at Sewanee.[11] He served as chaplain from July 17, 1871, until July 30, 1883. While at Sewanee he taught a variety of courses to both undergraduates and theological students, including Hebrew, exegesis, New Testament language and interpretation, Old Testament language and interpretation, homiletics, and systematic divinity.[12]

In April 1873, DuBose's wife, "Nannie," died. On December 18, 1878, DuBose married his second wife, Maria Louise Yerger. She and Hattie B. Kells had moved their school for women from Jackson, Mississippi, to Monteagle, Tennessee, with DuBose's help. This school was chartered as Fairmount College, and DuBose served as its chaplain. It was about six miles from Sewanee. Maria died in 1887.

At the University of the South, DuBose was charged with organizing the first Theological Department. In 1877, the Theological Department was listed as a distinct school of the University of the South. The Theological Department, later called the School of Theology, was formally established in 1878. DuBose served as acting dean of the School of Theology after the death of his predecessor on September 11, 1893. DuBose was the second dean of the School of Theology from July 31, 1894, until his retirement on June 24, 1908.[13] He was dean emeritus until his death on August 18, 1918.[14]

DuBose's writing did cause some controversy. A reviewer of his *High Priesthood and Sacrifice* for the *Church of Ireland Gazette* notes that "his statements are a bit startling now and then."[15] A reviewer of J. O. F. Murray's

DuBose as a Prophet of Unity warns that "the danger of the Nestorian heresy is so ever menacing in a humanitarian age like the present that all language which seems to imply that the Lord of Glory was not only Man but a man, an individual Jew, is greatly to be deprecated." This reviewer notes that DuBose's teaching was "always most stimulating," but that "it must be received at some central points with caution."[16]

Ralph Luker notes that Professor Francis A. Shoup, a faculty colleague of DuBose, was rumored to be seeking a heresy trial for DuBose after he published *Soteriology*. Similarly, in 1894, DuBose's selection as second dean of the School of Theology was resisted by the bishop of Florida and the bishop of Georgia who "suggested that DuBose's theology was so unorthodox as to verge on heresy." Thomas F. Gailor, bishop of Tennessee, defended DuBose. Further discussion revealed that one of the objecting bishops had read nothing more than a review of *Soteriology*, and the other had read only one chapter of it. DuBose was elected dean despite their objections.[17]

DuBose hoped to see the influence of his theology in the life of the church. He told his former student Silas McBee, "what is to be desired is a *Movement* towards the Theology & Philosophy of which I am recognized as an Exponent."[18] Unfortunately, such a movement was not forthcoming in the terms that DuBose seemed to desire. It may be that the human tragedy of World War I and the disillusionment that followed in its wake led to a climate that was not receptive to the ecumenical optimism and "constructive" spirit of DuBose's vision.

However, many of DuBose's ideals were given expression in the *Constructive Quarterly: A Journal of the Faith, Work, and Thought of Christendom*. This journal was established in March 1913 and edited by Silas McBee. DuBose's commitment to ecumenism was reflected in his active role as a contributor to this ecumenical quarterly, which was devoted to "positive and constructive Christianity."[19] Eleven articles by DuBose were published in the *Constructive Quarterly* between 1913 and 1920. His last article, "The Faith of a Christian Today," was written in February 1918 and revised shortly before his death on August 18, 1918.[20] He published more articles in the journal than any other author.[21] DuBose's eleven articles in the *Constructive Quarterly* were republished in 1957 as *Unity in the Faith*, edited by W. Norman Pittenger. DuBose also served as a member of the editorial board of the *Constructive Quarterly* and contributed the lead article for its first issue. In this article, "A Constructive Treatment of Christianity," DuBose (in a characteristic word-play) began by defining "constructive" in terms of "construing." He states his "own construction, or construing, of Christianity" to be "that among us all, or all who will call themselves Christians, there will be a consensus or agreement, a unity, of faith and experience, so far as I shall express these, in comparison with which our differences ought to count as nothing."[19]

It is interesting to note that reaction against DuBose strained the ecumenical ties of the *Constructive Quarterly*. Roman Catholic scholars Leonce de Grandmaison and Pierre Batiffol protested against DuBose's articles "Christ the Revelation of God" and "The Subjective and Objective in Religion," and withdrew from editorial involvement in the *Constructive Quarterly*. Grandmaison could "absolutely neither admit nor tolerate" DuBose's "modernist" argument. Grandmaison said that DuBose seemed to represent authentic Christianity, but in a way that was "very largely independent of traditional, objective dogmatic doctrines."[23]

From August 2 to August 6, 1911, to commemorate the fortieth anniversary of DuBose's coming to Sewanee, there was a reunion of his former students at the university. The *Churchman* noted the variety of perspectives represented by DuBose's students at the reunion, and observed, "In miniature, the DuBose reunion illustrated Dr. DuBose's philosophy."[24] DuBose's philosophy, with its emphasis on the value of experience, was not sectarian—high church and low church theologies received equal respect in his classroom—leading to the diversity remarked by the *Churchman*. The autobiographical papers DuBose read to his former students at the morning sessions of the reunion became part of his book *Turning Points in My Life*.

The reunion was the fullest public recognition in DuBose's lifetime of the personal and theological contribution he had made. It was also the first time DuBose publicly told of his conversion as a cadet. He admitted, "I have always spoken from myself, but I have never spoken of myself."[25] Certainly, the reunion was itself a turning point for DuBose, along with those he described in his book.

DuBose's emphasis on the role of experience in the process of salvation underscores the theological significance of *Turning Points*. Indeed, DuBose's spiritual autobiography was *the* major theological publication that revealed and developed his theological method in terms of the central role of human experience. This position is not shared by Donald S. Armentrout, who acknowledges only six works "of major theological importance" by DuBose.[26] In a review of Alexander's collection of DuBose's writings, Armentrout even refers to "DuBose's six published books."[27] Armentrout includes no selection from *Turning Points* in his anthology, stating that *Turning Points* "was not a substantial theological work but was much more autobiographical and personal."[28] It *was* autobiographical and personal. It tells the story of DuBose's

life relative to his experiences of conversion, suffering, discovery, and transformation. However, DuBose's theological development of autobiographical and personal details in *Turning Points* also provides the key to
understanding the experiential basis of his theological method.

J. O. F. Murray begins his discussion of DuBose with *Turning Points*
and "The Background of Spiritual Experience," followed shortly by consideration of "His Method—Spiritual Psychology."[29] Murray acknowledges
that DuBose's thought was embodied in "seven volumes published between
1892 and 1911," along with his *Constructive Quarterly* articles.[30] It is no coincidence that Murray recognizes the importance of experience in DuBose's
theological method, and counts *Turning Points* among DuBose's seven volumes of theology.

Turning Points was a major theological work, akin to Augustine's *Confessions*. It spells out "the presence and vitality of the Word of God" in
DuBose's life. The central role of human experience in his theological
method comes across even more clearly here than in his other theological
writings because he uses the personal details of his conversion, suffering,
discovery, and transformation as the experiential basis for his theological
reflection. While his experiences of suffering and loss are implicitly related
to his understanding of christology and the cross, DuBose explicitly relates
his experiences of conversion and transformation to his soteriology—his
understanding of salvation. Likewise, he draws out the relationship between
his experiences of discovery and his ecclesiological understanding of the
need for openness in the church.

DUBOSE'S EXPERIENCES OF LOSS

It was toward the end of the Civil War, after the Confederate defeat at the
battle of Cedar Creek in Virginia, that DuBose had a moment of shock and
realization. That night his brigade slept behind a line of battle for the first
time in the war. At this moment he realized the impossibility of success for
the Confederate cause and the world he had known all his life. He "felt as
if everything was gone!"[31] When he faced the fact that the Confederacy was
"beginning to break" after the "disgraceful rout" of his side at Cedar Creek,
"the end of the world was upon me as completely as upon the Romans when
the barbarians had overrun them." With respect to his moment of recognition "under the stars" that the Confederate cause was lost, DuBose states
that "such an experience can never be altogether lost, and I go back to it at
times for such a sense of the utter extinction of the world, and presence of

only the Eternal and the Abiding, as is seldom vouchsafed to one." He recalls that "the actual issue was all upon me that fateful night in which, under the stars, alone upon the planet, without home or country or any earthly interest of object before me, my very world at an end, I redevoted myself wholly and only to God, and to the work and life of His Kingdom, whatever and wherever that might be."[32] For DuBose, this was a moment of rededication to God and God's purposes.

Adding to his burden, his mother and father died during the war, his father from measles, which he caught from sick soldiers he was ministering to on a train. There was considerable suffering in DuBose's neighborhood as well. A close family friend, Mrs. Haskell, heard in a single day of the death of her brother and two sons. Both the sons had been DuBose's roommates. He named his son William Haskell DuBose after the brother who had attended the University of Virginia. DuBose's home church, St. John's in Winnsboro, was severely damaged in Sherman's raid. According to one account, the church was "wantonly burned," and its organ, furniture, books, and church bell were destroyed.[33]

After the Civil War, DuBose returned home to great desolation: "widows and bereaved persons were at every turn, and worst of all, facing us everywhere was the loss of our country." Living conditions were "for some years no better than in war." He found that "the country was stript of the barest means of subsistence; our social and political condition was unendurable and hopeless." Although wealthy before the war, his family was "utterly impoverished" after the war ended. His family home had "lain in the centre of Sherman's famous march." South Carolina was a dangerous place after the Civil War. The "carpet bag regime was at its height and its worst." DuBose recalled this to be a time of lawlessness, fear, and exploitation by those in power. "Barns and sometimes homes were burned by night." On one occasion his own home, the church rectory, was entered at night by a robber who was discovered in the bedroom where DuBose's daughter Susie and other relatives were sleeping.[34]

The succeeding years brought additional losses. In the early summer of 1872, after DuBose was elected chaplain and professor of moral science, his wife and three children joined him at Sewanee. That fall, when his fourth child, Samuel, was born, his wife's health began to fail. DuBose believed that Nannie "never did recover from certain hardships endured during the war, for she was so utterly unselfish, and thoughtful of all except herself, that she impaired her health." She died in April 1873. Samuel died in the spring of 1874, after lingering for some time following a severe bronchial attack. The intense pain of Samuel's death was still present to DuBose years later when he dictated his "Reminiscences" to his son Haskell. He recalled, "I used to carry him in my arms and he loved it. He died. I miss that little boy to this day. I miss him *now*."[35]

DuBose learned, however, that experiences of loss could provide the occasion for human openness toward and dependence upon God. His experiences also taught him the importance of poverty in the life of faith. He explains in *Turning Points*, "The principle of prayer is rooted in the fact of need, want, poverty. Our Lord makes poverty the first condition of spiritual blessedness, because in it begins all that dependence upon God the end of which is oneness with Him. Out of that poverty come all godly sorrow, all noble meekness and humility, all hunger and thirst for rightness and fulness of life, all faith in God, all hope in self, all true self-realization and soul satisfaction."[36] The emptiness of poverty can lead to the openness of heart that is filled by the love of God.

DuBose's experiences of loss were formative for his understanding of the role of the cross in the life of Jesus, and in the Christian life. He urges in his Transfiguration sermon at the DuBose reunion: ". . . the fact that even our Lord, in the needful and inevitable infirmity of our present humanity, had moments in which He needed to know anew that He was the Son of God, that He had to learn afresh upon the very cross that there is no such thing as a divine forsaking, though so often there seems to be, ought to teach us how to have faith in even our darkest hours, and hope when we are faintest and farthest off."[37] Through his darkest hours and most painful losses he came to experience that there is no divine forsaking. It was as true for him in the face of defeat and destruction in war as it was for Jesus on the cross.

DuBose's experiences of loss were also formative for his understanding of the role of poverty and the cross in the Christian life, and in christology. He asks, rhetorically, in his Transfiguration sermon, "For what is Jesus Christ but God in us and we in God? And what is the Cross but the actual process by which all that is not God dies in us, and all that is lives and grows in us?"[38] In his address on "The Theology of the Child," he notes, "only he who knows the Cross knows redemption and resurrection and eternal life."[39] DuBose knew the cross and its benefits through his experiences of loss.

DuBose's Experiences of Transformation

When DuBose was just eighteen and a cadet at The Citadel, he had his first mystical experience of conversion. After a long march, DuBose and two other cadets attended a "roaring farce of a play" and then spent the night in a hotel. After the others were asleep, DuBose got up to pray. He later recalled this experience: "Perfectly unconscious and unsuspicious of anything unusual, I knelt to go through the form, when of a sudden there swept over me a feeling of the emptiness and unmeaningness of the act and of my whole life and self. I leapt to my feet trembling, and then that happened which I can only describe by saying that a light shone about me and a Presence filled the room. At the same time an ineffable joy and peace took possession of me which it is impossible either to express or explain."[40] With respect to his experience of "youthful conversion," DuBose later stated that "there was nothing there, in consciousness, but God and myself; but that was a new light, a new world, a new life, and a new self."[41]

In his "Reminiscences," he recalls that "a new presence had come into my life and it was so absolute and positive, there was no mistaking it." He was afraid to go to sleep that night, "lest it disappear," but the sense of the presence was with him the next day and thereafter.[42]

For DuBose, this moment of conversion was an experience of the otherness and presence of God that ultimately defied description. He notes that its "lack of explicitness" was striking, since "so little was there in it of the definite and defined features of Christianity, that it would scarcely seem to have been as yet distinctively Christian."[43]

He returned to his "natural habits and duties" after this experience, but "the form which the intervening change in me assumed was mainly that of a sensitized and transfigured—not only consciousness, but—conscience."[44] He spent the rest of the year "consolidating" his gains, and determined to study for the ordained ministry. Perhaps because public discussion of such an experience may have seemed unusual to many in the Episcopal Church of his day, where order and form were often emphasized to the detriment of "personal religion," DuBose mentioned it to no one until the reunion with his students, some fifty years later. And yet, he says of the experience, "it has been all that time present with me."[45] It was for him "a life-long matter of scientific as well as religious interest to analyze and understand that experience."[46]

However powerful the moment of conversion was for DuBose, it was the beginning—not the completion—of a new life. "There was then no conscious sense of sin, nor repentance, nor realization of the meaning of the Cross, or of the Resurrection, or of the Church or the Sacraments, nor indeed of the Incarnation or of Christ Himself. What then was there?—There was simply a New World without me, and a New Self in me—in both which for the first time, visibly, sensibly, really, God was."[47]

DuBose did not grasp all the realities of the Christian faith in their entirety at the moment of his conversion. His was an "already, but not yet" situation: "The task of materializing or actualizing that as yet only ideal, of embodying the sentiment of it into habit and character and life, I was indeed far enough from realizing. But were not the principle and the potency of the whole already present and operative in me?"[48] Although the reality of God's saving presence was already present to him, fully and objectively, he had not yet made it his own. That was to be the work of his lifetime.

DuBose's conversion experience seems to have been the basis for his distinction between God's objective reality and the subjective and saving reality of our faith. He states, ". . . there is a great deal which we may outwardly confess as *the faith*, which we rightly hold on the reasonable external authority of corporate and historical Christianity, which nevertheless to be compelled to profess, as in its totality our personal subjective actual and attained faith, would simply involve us in either self-deception or hypocrisy."[49] The difference between the *objective truth for a person* and the *realized truth of a person* calls for "the life-time process, as one can, of gradually digesting, assimilating, and converting that faith into one's own, and finding in it the full food and content of one's life."[50] For example, DuBose understood baptism in terms of an objective gift that was to be followed by a lifetime of realization. "Baptism is not an act of man which his faith goes before and accomplishes, it is an act of God which his faith comes after and accepts and appropriates and realizes or actualizes in himself."[51] In an objective sense, the newly baptized person is a Christian and a full member of the church. But the claiming, appropriating, and making subjectively real of that identity will involve the rest of the person's life.

This process of converting the faith into one's own involves many experiences and their interpretation—not just one experience at the inception of faith. The truth of the saving process is known experientially. It was known for DuBose in his own awareness of self. He explains, "My proof, I may say my verification, of the fact of God's coming to me, apart from all the mystery of the way, may be expressed in this simple truth of experience, that in finding Him I found myself: a man's own self, when he has once truly come to himself, is his best and only experimental proof of God. The act of the Prodigal's 'coming to himself' was also that of his arising and returning to his Father."[52] Similarly, in his paper "Liberty and Authority in Christian Truth," DuBose warned, "A truth and life which are only the Church's and are not in actual and active process of becoming our own and wholly our own, are much worse than nothing to us; a salvation which does not save becomes our condemnation."[53] The saving process is actualized as reality in our lives.

DuBose's soteriology was formed by his experiences and relationships. His father had a strong influence in his life. He expected DuBose to "take a full collegiate course and a professional training afterward."[54] DuBose's father often "did the hard thing" for him, prompting him to take courses in the areas of study where he was least strong. When DuBose became homesick as a third year cadet at The Citadel, his father detected the change in him from his letters. DuBose's father wrote him a letter that was "like a *lash*," which woke him and stirred him up from his homesickness.[55] Acknowledging his father's influence, DuBose explained that "almost every letter of his came as a sort of impact on my life." DuBose received another important letter from his father at about the time he was leaving seminary to join the Confederate Army at the beginning of the Civil War. DuBose was torn between the choices of staying in seminary or joining the army. Although his father obviously favored the course of joining the army, he said that his children "deferred to his wishes almost too readily," and he "had never wished to impair their freedom." DuBose understood this letter from his father "to commend my act in following my own judgment rather than his wishes in this particular matter," although his father did express "relief and pleasure at my somewhat belated patriotism." DuBose described this letter as "a turning-point" which lived in his memory.[56] Certainly his father encouraged him to do his own thinking and to have the courage to act on his convictions. This influence may well be seen in the unswerving freedom in seeking the truth that characterizes DuBose's theological method.

DuBose's soteriology was even more strongly influenced by his own experience which led him to appreciate how the objective gift of God's presence may increasingly be appropriated and realized subjectively in the life of the believer. DuBose believes in a transformative and saving fulfillment in Christ that makes the fundamental difference in human life—a "difference" that is known experientially.

DuBose's Experiences of Discovery

During his academic career as a student and a teacher, DuBose experienced discovery through his openness to the truth and his critical evaluation of all kinds of ideas, perspectives, and positions. These experiences were formative for his life and theology, especially his vision for the church.

In October 1859, DuBose entered the diocesan seminary in Camden, South Carolina, where he encountered a senior student who had strong Calvinistic and low-churchmanship views. DuBose recalled that this "intelligent and aggressive theological student . . . had gone to Princeton to find there under the Hodges and Alexanders of that day meat strong enough for his spiritual pabulum."[57] This seminarian challenged DuBose in terms of his knowledge of Greek and St. Paul as to "whether the language and argument of St. Paul did not necessitate all the essential principles, the five points, of Calvinism." This encounter required DuBose to face and overcome his own prejudices, and commit himself to "follow the truth wherever it may lead me." It was a turning point that caused DuBose "difficulties and perplexities" for "several years to come."[58]

For DuBose, the issue had much to do with openness to the possibility of finding the truth despite his preconceived ideas: ". . . at the time I encountered and had to overcome this temptation: We are often enough tempted to believe what antecedent prejudice or inclination makes us wish to believe. . . . I asked myself, Am I prepared to make the necessary sacrifice in order to follow the truth wherever it may lead me? And I came near identifying that query with this one, Am I strong enough and selfless enough to accept Calvinism? Whereas it should have been this, Am I open and prepared to accept Calvinism if it is indeed, and I fairly find it to be, the truth?"[59] Once he had faced and considered Calvinism with an open mind, he found that he was not obliged to "revert" to Calvinism. But this experience, prompted by the challenge of a student with views that differed from his own, was for DuBose "the first thing that touched and really set going the forward movement of life and thought in me."[60] It was a question of committing himself in openness to the truth. It involved his personal, spiritual, and academic integrity.

The resolution of his "difficulties and perplexities" regarding Calvinism had "results in all my future thinking and teaching." The "permanent profit of that experience" was that he came away from it as "a life-long student and companion of St. Paul's faith and life," which really determined his "whole subsequent character and career."[61] All these benefits, including his "discovery" of St. Paul's importance, resulted from DuBose's willingness to follow the truth wherever it would lead him. Because he was not bound by the prejudices that he brought to the original question of Calvinism, he experienced the values of openness and fair testing of ideas relative to Christian belief.

DuBose also experienced openness and discovery in his teaching at Sewanee. There was a spirit of free inquiry for discussion in his classes. He explains, "Everything was to be tested and verified, according to our Lord's prescription, in the light and in the terms of human nature, human life, and human destiny. All that was true for us ought to be true to us, and would be if we were in a state and attitude of correspondence with the truth. To establish this correspondence was our task."[62] DuBose did not use old notes or manuscripts, preferring to approach "every day and every year anew, without any help from the past through any records of my own."[63] Theodore Bratton, one of DuBose's students who later became the bishop of Mississippi, states that this approach was "altogether revolutionary in its departure from the stern, set forms of the time."[64]

It was out of this environment that DuBose's published theology emerged. He recalled, "Questions that arose within the class began to spread without the class, and the time came when it became necessary to make known my teaching to a larger audience." It was his students "who in loving compulsion forced the publication of my first book, and have been behind as well in all the rest." DuBose's students were "*in*" his books because the dynamic of his classroom was formative for him as well as for them. He notes, "I was in fact more one of them than one merely over them. I was finding and making myself in and with and through and by, as well as upon, them."[65] This process is echoed by Bratton, who stated, "The Doctor's students of the decade of 1880 to 1890 used to think and say, with no little pride, that the writing of the Soteriology was inspired by their inquiring minds, bristling with questions suggested by his lectures."[66]

The result of DuBose's theological method of open inquiry was visible in his former students who attended the reunion in his honor. They represented all the pieties and interpretations in the Episcopal Church. There were no "DuBosians." But there were many who had been furthered and formed in their own development and thinking through encounter with DuBose as their teacher. With respect to them, DuBose states, "the gathering is made up, not of those of one way, but of those of all the ways of thinking and believing in the Church. No one thinks of asking which way is most or least in evidence among us, because, with whatever of differences, we have learned here to think and live together without sense or recognition of parties or partisanship. All honest and reasonable difficulties or convictions have been met and treated with equal interest, sympathy, and mutual respect and understanding."[67] DuBose's idealism concerning his gathered former students is understandable. Nevertheless, he clearly saw in them the potential of a church where members of different perspectives could share in living and discerning the truth. His students were the living witness to the open forum that was his vision for the church.

An example of such "differences" within the church is "expressed by the two terms *Evangelical* and *Catholic*," which DuBose discusses in his *Constructive Quarterly* essay "Evangelical and Catholic: Each Needs the Other, Both Need the Church, and the Church Needs Both." He notes that "each of these terms . . . has become the designation of a 'party' in the church, almost synonymous with Catholic and Protestant in the wider field of Christianity."[68] In response to an evangelical tendency to emphasize the subjective in religion, and a catholic tendency to emphasize the objective in religion, DuBose urges a position of synthesis. The "sincere and religious 'Catholic,' however he may cling to and make much of what we may call the 'externals' of his religion, cannot be assumed to be not as much alive to all the subjective implications of it—faith, conversion, personal piety, etc.—as the earnest Evangelical is to all the objective presuppositions and grounds of his own subjectivity." Instead, "the truly Evangelical as necessarily presupposes all the real Catholic, as the latter necessarily issues in the former." DuBose urges much more than the *tolerance* of a "consent 'to live and let live.'" The respective "sides" or perspectives need each other for mutual completion in the church.[69]

The openness DuBose called for was at the heart of his theological method for discerning truth by individual Christians and by the church. He believed it could work in the church because he had seen it work in his classroom for forty years, where his "place and part was in the mine, not in the mint, of the truth of Christianity, that free enquiry and investigation, not dogma (which would have its proper place after) was in order with us."[70] With respect to this method, DuBose notes, "I believe that I always felt that scepticism and criticism were inevitable instruments of truth and righteousness and life, and that nothing in this world was proved, tested, or verified that had not passed through them to the uttermost end and limit."[71] The open forum that he called for in the church was at the heart of his ecclesiology.

It was DuBose's strong conviction that the church should not fear the truth, nor should the church fear a process of free and open inquiry for the sake of truth. On the contrary, the church would ultimately be aided and strengthened by truth wherever discovered, and by the correcting or unmasking of any falsehood. Perceiving no "chasm" between natural and supernatural truth, DuBose was unafraid of the scientific method and the discoveries of science.

In fact, the church's quest for truth could be furthered by the rigor of critical thought as used in the scientific method of his day, and in biblical criticism. "This is an age in which everything must stand or fall by its own internal virtue of reality. Professions and pretensions must go down before the true and wholesome spirit of scepticism, criticism, and verification which will spare nothing as too sacred for it, and which is most needed just in the things that are the most sacred. The only thing on God's earth that is going to escape or survive the winnowing fan, the refiner's fire, that Christianity above all things ought to be and is, is the thing, whatever it is, that is genuine, that is real."[72] DuBose was unafraid to question and test the reality of the most sacred assumptions in matters of faith.

The open forum in the church would be the best means for discerning the genuine, the true, and the real. Likewise, the open forum would enable members of different perspectives to live together and grow in faith and understanding. The concept of the open forum at the heart of DuBose's ecclesiology was derived from his experiences of discovery as a student and teacher.

EXPERIENCE, FAITH, AND THEOLOGICAL METHOD

George Townshend, who wrote an article in the *Churchman* about the DuBose reunion, notes that the autobiographical sketches DuBose presented were "a frank and clear revelation of a striking personality." Townshend explains that "in these last words the doctor, in a series of set papers, lived his life over again for the benefit of his hearers, narrated for them the most vital of his experiences and explained the lessons which he himself had learned from them."[73]

Townshend's description of the presentations by DuBose offers an important insight into the heart of his theological method: his theology was based in and formed by the experiences he lived. Furthermore, DuBose's method was meant to be tested in light of the experiences of his readers and hearers.

DuBose notes that "essential truths" like the truth of Jesus Christ or the truth of immortality "are their own best if not only proofs," and that "apart from actual and adequate life and experience they can never be logically or speculatively demonstrated."[74] He urges that "the final and only convincing proof of religion is the experience of what will perfect and complete human life."[75] Similarly, the things of the life of the spirit "cannot be known by proofs; they can be proved only by knowing."[76] We can verify the truth of religion only by "actual experiment or experience of it. We must live it in order to know it."[77] DuBose thus emphasizes the experiential nature of spiritual knowledge. He explained to his former students at the reunion: "I think I may say that whatever of inspiration or illumination ever came to you through my life or teaching, came through the fact that I presented Christ and Christianity at first hand, not in the letter but in the spirit, not in traditional or conventional forms or technical language, but in living terms of actual human relation and experience."[78] Human experience is most relevant for DuBose in the life of faith and the work of theology. In his theology he seeks to share the spiritual truths of his own experience, and to engage and explain the spiritual realities of others' lives.

It is noteworthy that DuBose's autobiography was not limited to religious experiences as such, but drew on the full range of his life. Through varied experiences he came to know God, and verified the reality of God's presence in his life. His autobiography also discloses how his earliest, essentially "unthematic" experience of "Presence" came to greater Christian realization throughout his life.

Experience is at the heart of his theology. He notes in *The Gospel in the Gospels* that instead of urging the "mere conventional language of Christianity," he "would if possible speak in the common language of common experience."[79] He states that during his four years of military service in the Civil War he "acquired the habit of combining thought with life and experience."[80] DuBose emphasizes that we know as we can in all areas of life, including the spiritual. He explains that "however God in any way or degree makes himself known to us, we may depend upon it that it is through our own way of knowing him."[81] Salvation operates "only through the natural and spiritual organs and activities of ourselves, our reason or intelligence, our affections and desires, our will, our acts and habits and character and life." Our "actual environment" provides the opportunity for salvation because our "actual experience is just what we need to become all ourselves in Christ."[82]

The discernment of divine truth is likewise based in experience. Truth ("whether of the natural or of the spiritual reason") is believed "because it is truth and not because it is proved." Those "ideas or sentiments of God, of immortality, of religious faith and worship" that are "true in themselves" will persist.[83] This intrinsic truth must be *perceptible* through experience. DuBose likewise urges that discerning God through experience is ultimately a corporate and not an individual task. The truth of God "must rest upon the true consensus of experience." It "cannot rest upon the variable experience of individuals."[84]

Experience also provides a necessary basis for theological understanding. The author of the Letter to the Hebrews is not primarily "interested even in priesthood or sacrifice," but in "the facts and truths of life and of experience, which he finds these the best figures for expressing." But, DuBose asks, how can the author of the Letter to the Hebrews "translate these mere figures or vehicles into truths of life and experience" for others "if they have no life or experience of their own for the apprehension of them." Therefore the "completeness or perfection of his exposition can only . . . go step by step with their progress in understanding, which is their growth in life."[85]

DuBose does not exclude or deny religious authority, proofs, or tradition, but he warns that religious truth must ring true to experience, no matter how fully authenticated it might be by proofs or tradition. In this sense, religious knowledge must proceed a posteriori from experience rather than taking the form of a priori conclusions relative to experience. DuBose urges, "not God himself nor Jesus Christ nor the Scriptures could sufficiently attest to us the truth of Christianity as our truth and our life if it were not equally attested as such by the spiritual common sense and experience of men always and everywhere."[86] Similarly, he notes that "while the truth of Christ is in one aspect absolute it is also in another sense relative to us and is to find its ultimate verification in the universal testimony of human reason and experience."[87] For DuBose, it is through reason and experience that we may know God and discern divine truth. In Aristotelian terms, DuBose considered that the "end" of the objective truth of salvation in Christ is in the subjective realization of that truth in our lives. That salvation must be true not only to us, but in us. For DuBose, the saving process was moved powerfully with his transformative experience of conversion as a cadet. But the realization of that process—the appropriating of the meaning of that experience—was the work of his lifetime. It involved many subsequent experiences of conversion, many "turning points" in his life.

DuBose's emphasis on experience comes from his understanding of the Incarnation. With respect to the prologue of the Gospel of John, DuBose notes, "'the Word of Life'—God Himself, Himself imparting— speaks to us, according to St. John's account of it, in the flesh: not through one sense only, but through all, through every natural avenue of human perception, knowledge, or experience."[88] DuBose observes that "nothing ever comes from God to man except through man, and except through the organs or faculties and laws of human transmission."[89] Our knowledge of God necessarily involves human experience.

For example, our experiences of human love can provide the basis for statements that truly signify the love of God. DuBose draws out an analogy between the human experience of falling in love and the inspiration and renewal of God's coming to us: "What we call 'falling in love' comes to us just as naturally and just as mysteriously and inexplicably as that other more spiritual experience of which the Lord says: 'The wind bloweth where it listeth, and thou hearest the sound thereof, but canst not tell whence it cometh or whither it goeth: so is every one that is born of the Spirit.'"[90] With respect to human love, DuBose concludes that "the man is made for the woman and the woman for the man, and neither is complete or satisfied without the other." Similarly, in proportional terms, the person is neither complete nor satisfied until the coming of the "divine love in which God makes Himself one with us." DuBose draws on the "ever new old words" of Augustine to explain this need: "my God Thou hast made me for Thyself, and my soul will find no rest, until it rest in Thee."[91]

It is important to note that DuBose drew upon the full range of his life experience in his theological method. He did not seek to isolate "pure" religious experience from the rest of his life. Although he clearly expressed the profound impact of his mystical conversion experience on his life, faith, and theology, he did not view that supernatural experience as an isolated phenomenon. In his autobiography, and in his life, the mystical and transcendent was an integral part of his entire experience. His autobiography chronicled the "turning *points*" of his life—including his mystical conversion experience, and numerous other experiences that were not distinctive in a mystical or supernatural way. Other turning points included, for example, his experiences of loss, adversity, and escape as a soldier; his "escape" from episcopal election in the Diocese of South Carolina; and his appointment at the University of the South and subsequent experiences of teaching. These were also significant for his faith development and theology, even though they were not distinctively mystical or supernatural.

DuBose's position that the entirety of our human experience may serve the purpose of our salvation is evident in his refusal to "compartmentalize" his distinctively mystical conversion from the rest of his life. We are to be saved *through*, not *from*, the conditions and experiences of human life in the world. DuBose notes that "life or salvation is not away from the natural to the spiritual, but through and by the natural into the spiritual." The "experiences of our life as it is" are "not only to be endured and survived, but recognized and used as divine means and instruments of our making and raising to the full stature of ourselves" in the process of salvation. Christ "brought God and heaven down into hearts and lives and conditions here—where they are most needed and therefore best acquired."[92]

DuBose's understandings of the cross, the process of conversion, and the needed openness of the church were formative for his christology, his soteriology, and his ecclesiology. All were rooted in his personal experiences of loss, transformation, and discovery. For DuBose, this was a matter of theological method. His story shared at the 1911 reunion discloses the "turning points" of the saving process in his life. DuBose's work of spiritual autobiography is thus the key to interpreting his theology. He sought to communicate the truths of faith and theology that were rooted in his life experience, so that others could understand and *live* the saving process he had known. DuBose presents the relation of theological reflection and pastoral life in a powerful way. He offers a theology of personally experienced salvation by sharing the saving lessons of his experience.

CHAPTER 2

Salvation

DuBose's theology is a systematic study of the process of salvation. As he considers *how* salvation is to be actualized in our own lives, he consistently emphasizes the importance of human experience in the saving process and in theological reflection. Subsequent chapters in this study will present DuBose's understanding of the Christ, the Spirit, and the church—especially with reference to their role in our salvation. This chapter provides an introduction to DuBose's soteriology, his theology of salvation, which is the heart of his theology, just as the system of theology which he develops in *Soteriology* is the paradigm for his published work. My consideration of DuBose's soteriology draws primarily on his book *The Soteriology of the New Testament*. DuBose was fifty-six when the first edition of *Soteriology* was published in 1892, and he declined to undertake a general revision of the book when a new edition was published in 1899. Although *Soteriology* was his first published book of theology, it reflects his mature theological thought.

THE REALITY AND REALIZATION OF SAVING EXPERIENCE

The Proof of Transformative Experience

DuBose's soteriology strongly reflects his emphasis on the role of experience in theology. First of all, salvation must be real. The reality of Christianity is not found in its consistency with tradition or in its appeals to authority, but in the *actual* salvation that it brings. A "salvation" that does not save is no salvation at all. DuBose urges that if "Christianity be not human Salvation, no authority of Creed or Scripture, no voice of God from heaven, will make it so or impose it finally as such upon the reason and the common sense of mankind."[1] Salvation, like all truths, is known through human experience

sion of our law, and death of ourselves, which we call the Fall" is "the *actual* condition of the nature which we all inherit."[18] Sin "is the negation or contradiction of holiness. Disunion, separation, enmity with God is thus an *actual* state of things."[19] Christ takes away the separation between God and humanity because "by His abolishment of sin He has *actually* brought humanity, both in His body natural and in His body mystical, into a real oneness with God."[20] We are "naturally spiritual" in that we are "by nature constituted for personal union with God," but one "is not actually spiritual until or unless he has *actually* entered into the union with God for which his nature has constituted him."[21] He likewise notes that "the gist and rub of life" consists "in the passage from passive impressions to active principles, in the conversion of ideas, sentiments, desires and purposes into *actual* habit and character and personality."[22] DuBose's use of the word "actually" emphasizes that he is describing realities of the human condition and spiritual life.

Our saving union with Christ whereby we share his victory over death in resurrection life is not merely an expression of spiritual truth; it is an actuality in our lives. DuBose urges that Christ is our reconciliation and "at-one-ment," the "actual personal oneness of God with man and man with God, which is in itself our spiritual good, and our only cure or Salvation from spiritual evil." Christ is our redemption, the "actual freedom of humanity from the bondage of sin and death, and its obedience to its true law of holiness and life, which is in itself man's moral good, and his only Salvation or emancipation from moral evil." Christ is our resurrection, the "actual raising or rising of humanity out of all such limitation, contradiction, and destruction of its true being and selfhood as is properly denominated death, which is in itself man's natural good and his only Salvation from natural evil."[23]

The reality of salvation that we may know is made possible through the divine initiative; God's initiative comes first, preceding our subjective realization of it. God "is not our Father because we are His children; but we are His children because He is our Father." This underscores the importance and reality of God's initiative in the saving process. DuBose notes that "we can love God only as He first loves us,"[24] and "we can make ourselves at one with God only as God first makes himself at one with us."[25] We depend on the divine initiative to know the reality of salvation in our lives.

It is especially through faith that we participate in the saving process. Of course, our faith would be of no avail if there were no objective gift of salvation to receive. Faith "does not create a fact, it only accepts one."[26] However, we must still subjectively accept the gift of salvation that is offered to us. An "objective divine revelation of truth or life is dependent upon and of no avail without a corresponding subjective human power of apprehension and acceptance."[27] Yet even our faith itself reflects God's initiative, and "is but the work of the grace which is God's part."[28] DuBose states that *"we actually begin to become spiritual only from the point when God's Spirit begins to work with ours through the working of ours with His."*[29] The completed process of salvation revealed in Jesus' life is to be *our* own reality in him. This process of salvation involves God's initiative, God's objective gift to us in Christ, God's subjective influence on us through the Holy Spirit, and our free cooperation and participation. The end of this saving process is our at-one-ment with God.

THE PROCESS OF SALVATION

The Already and Not Yet of Salvation

DuBose understands salvation in terms of a process, a progressive reality that is already and actually completed in Christ, and that has begun in us insofar as we now live in Christ and he lives in us. "We are saved in Jesus Christ in whom salvation is complete," he urges, "even though we are not saved in ourselves in whom we know that it is very far from complete." Christianity is thus "nothing less" than God incarnate in us "in and through" Jesus "as to be actually and personally, though humanly and progressively, our Holiness, our Righteousness, and our Life."[30] This process is not yet actualized, but it is completed *in faith* through the impartation of life in Christ. Faith "in the Word of God is a present possession of future things." DuBose likewise notes the "forereaching power of faith, to see the end already in the beginning and to possess the gift in the promise."[31] In "the action of divine grace operating through our faith," we are "already where Christ is and what Christ is."[32] Similarly, "God so surely makes things what they are by his word, that his word already calls things that are not yet as though they already were."[33]

Our condition relative to salvation may be characterized as "already but not yet." The divine redemption and righteousness in Christ "is in one sense *already* given to us, and *already* ours; and it is in another sense *not yet* given to us, nor ours."[34] DuBose explains, ". . . in faith and in its language all that is true of Christ is said of us; we are all that he has become, risen, ascended, complete, blessed with all spiritual blessing in heavenly places. But it is only in faith that this is wholly already true; in fact, it is not yet so; it is only wholly *to be* true.[35]" By faith we may *already* know and share the completion of salvation in Christ that is *not yet* ours in accomplished fact.

DuBose notes, "everything that is to be ours in fact in Christ is already ours in faith in Him."[36] In this regard, the publican in Jesus' parable was justified by faith, because "God accepts in us that elementary condition and beginning of all righteousness which He sees in our initial faith, as our sole part in the then relations between us."[37]

Our participation in this process of salvation whereby our "not yet" increasingly becomes our "already" is only through union with Christ, so that his life increasingly becomes ours, and our life increasingly becomes his. DuBose warns, *"we* can neither know, nor have, nor incarnate, God's Word or Spirit save as these have incarnated themselves in humanity in Jesus Christ and incarnate themselves in us as incorporate in the humanity, or members of the body, of Jesus Christ."[38]

This "process of gradual becoming" will involve God's initiative and grace, and our cooperation by faith.[39] DuBose explains that "Faith in the righteousness and life of Christ assimilates and transforms us into the likeness of Christ's righteousness and life."[40] We begin and continue the process in Christ, by the Holy Spirit, following and sharing in Christ's process of human holiness, righteousness and life.

"Progressive Salvation" can involve a lifetime of experience that begins from birth. Our relationship with God "undergoes evolution and growth through what in the experience of life God and man become to each other."[41] We are not saved by faith *from* human experience; we are saved *through* human experience and our relationship with God. Our salvation, our life in Christ, "can come only in conjunction, in reaction, in conflict and strife with human environment as it is and with all human conditions as they are."[42] Our perfection, whether natural or spiritual, is "attainable only by stages." Sanctification "at the best is a gradual and lifelong process" because our spiritual faculties are "subject to the law of growth" and "progressive in their functions."[43]

Our salvation is worked out through our experiences and choices, which are therefore integral to the saving process. The "way" of salvation involves a lifetime of experiences, as it did for Jesus. DuBose explains, "I am not *I* in all the completeness of my idea and meaning from the moment of my conception or my birth. I may be potentially, but I certainly am not actually so."[44] Salvation was not complete in Jesus at his conception or birth, but only through his lived human holiness, righteousness, and life.

For now, we see the process completed only in Jesus, who lived out and embodies the salvation that will be ours by grace through faith. DuBose states, "As the Epistle to the Hebrews expresses it: 'We see *not yet* ourselves, but we see him' complete in all that constitutes a real human Salvation and redemption. But His completion means, and it has no meaning *unless* it means *ours*. He is what we shall be."[45] Thus, the not yet saved in us will be saved. DuBose explains that "while in the grace of God and in our faith our reconciliation is viewed as completed in Jesus Christ—*in fact*, it will only be completed when in Christ *we* shall be dead to the sin that separates us from God and alive in the holiness which is the only real reconciliation with Him."[46] The completion of the saving process is our at-one-ment with God, when all obstacles to God are removed and salvation is realized in our lives.

Nevertheless, the completion of our salvation is imputed to us even now by faith. DuBose explains that "where our faith truly answers to the divine grace, we are to God even as Jesus Christ Himself is, in whom He already sees us." The beginning of our repentance, and the beginning of our holiness and righteousness in Christ, is thus "received and treated as being righteousness." DuBose explains, "that which faith already appropriates as its own, God's grace goes beyond our faith in imputing to us as already our own."[47] We can know the life of Christ *now* by faith, by the imputed completion of the saving process, even though Jesus Christ is "as yet only the end of purpose, and infinitely not yet the end of attainment" in our lives.[48] Nevertheless, we may enjoy "already the peace of the faith which brings distant things near and makes future things present."[49] Our completed salvation in Christ will become an increasing reality as we continue in the saving process.

The Subjective Realization of Salvation

The "not yet" of our process of salvation will be "already" complete when objective salvation in Christ is subjectively realized in us. With respect to this divine redemption and righteousness, DuBose explains, "objectively, it is *given*, and therefore truly ours; subjectively, it is not yet *received*, and therefore not yet truly ours."[50] For DuBose, salvation in Christ is objectively ours already in the gift, but it is not yet subjectively ours until the process of salvation is realized in our lives. In this regard, I completely disagree with B. B. Warfield's incredible statement in a book review that DuBose expounds "a doctrine of purely subjective salvation."[51]

DuBose uses the parable of the prodigal son to illustrate the objective and subjective aspects of the saving process. He notes that the prodigal son really wanted "an internal or subjective reconciliation and restoration to unity with his father." But the "gradual healing and growth of internal and real unity" and "the subjective spirit of sonship" required first a restoration of the objective "external status of father and son."[52] In terms of our salvation, DuBose states that "the function of faith is not to cause but to accept and receive regeneration."[53]

When he explained regeneration in terms of objective gift and subjective realization, DuBose was dealing with one of the most hotly contested theological issues in the Episcopal Church of the nineteenth century. High Church Episcopalians stressed regeneration in terms of the "objective" covenant and grace of baptism, while Evangelical Episcopalians stressed the need for a "subjective" adult renewal of faith for regeneration. Dispute over use of the words "regenerate" and "regeneration" in the baptismal liturgy of the Episcopal Church led to an ecclesiastical trial of an Episcopal priest, and an eventual schism from the church.[54] DuBose draws together the truth of both positions, despite their apparent opposition. He describes regeneration in a way that acknowledges both the objective gift of regeneration in Christ and our subjective need to realize the gift of regeneration in our lives by faith.

But there is more to this process than just our belief. It concerns our actual saving transformation in Christ so that our real identity is *changed* through union with him. DuBose states, "Now this, *our being reconciled* to God, no doubt means that we are to accept in faith the fact of an objective reconciliation in Christ. But it does not mean that *only;* it means that we are to receive through faith the fact of a subjective reconciliation also, so as not only *to have been made one* but *to be one* with God in Christ."[55] Our at-one-ment with God in Christ is the fulfilment and meaning of the saving process.

The progressive movement from objective in Christ to increasing subjective realization of Christ has its own completion when our salvation is as objective and factual as Christ's. DuBose notes that "it is Jesus Christ our righteousness in faith, that makes Jesus Christ to become our righteousness in fact."[56] He likewise notes that "everywhere the business or function of spiritual or personal life is to convert meaning into reality, potentiality into actuality."[57] Though not yet perfected, as we subjectively realize the objective gift of Christ's life already given to us, the process of salvation becomes increasingly present in our lives.

PARTICIPATION, FREEDOM, AND MUTUALITY

Our Participation in Christ's Salvation

Salvation is not just in Christ, and it is certainly not just in us. Our hope is only in our sharing of the reconciliation, redemption, and resurrection that are available for us; actual spirituality "is consummated only in that personal union in which *we* become one with God as well as God with us."[58] DuBose notes in *The Gospel in the Gospels* that we are insufficient in ourselves to put away our sin. But this insufficiency "does not absolve us from the obligation of ourselves working out our complete and eternal destinies"; it "only implies that we can do so only in conjunction with something else."[59] This "something else" is our participation in Christ.

Salvation is in Christ *and* in us as we participate in the life of Christ. DuBose states that the "blood of Jesus Christ cleanseth us from all sin, because we are dead to sin by participation in His death and alive to holiness through experience of the power of His resurrection."[60] He thus urges a "blood theology" by which we share in the saving benefits of Christ's life and sacrifice. Jesus' human righteousness "was a righteousness, of which His 'blood' was the sole condition, and is the only symbol."[61] We die to sin "only by participation, by grace through faith, in Christ's death to sin. We are saved, not by our ability to die in the flesh and raise ourselves to life in the spirit, but only by the imparted grace and power of Christ's death and resurrection, which, however, when imparted, become our own actual death and resurrection."[62] Participation in Christ's life/death/resurrection necessarily involves us in sacrifice.

In terms of this blood theology, DuBose draws on the imagery of the Letter to the Hebrews to note that blood is "coincident" with the rending of the veil of separation between humanity and God. Accordingly, he states in *High Priesthood and Sacrifice* that "it is only through the rent veil, it is only with blood, that we can pass from ourselves into God." Everything that comes between us and God must likewise "be rent, though the rending be with blood."[63]

For Jesus, as for us, the "transition from sin to holiness, from death to life" is a passage that "cannot be made without blood, or otherwise than through death" because the way of at-one-ment with God "is by blood," and cannot "be completed or perfected without it." Jesus, "in His natural humanity," was "subject to the condition upon which alone we can come to God."[64] DuBose emphasizes this blood theology in *The Reason of Life* by drawing on imagery from important events in Jesus' life. Jesus' baptism in the River Jordan "signifies, involves, and promises the death to sin and life to God." But "the water of Jordan means, and finds its fulfilment only in, the blood of Calvary, the actual and complete death to sin and life to God."[65] Likewise, "the Wilderness, the Garden, and the Cross teach us clearly enough that the work of the spirit, the strife against sin, is won only by resistance unto blood, is finished only in death."[66] Our condition for coming to God is "nothing short of the absolute and complete one of dying in our mere nature, dying to ourselves, in order to live to God"; "there is no salvation, at least no human salvation, possible save through death."[67]

Death has a necessary place in the process of salvation. We are called to "infinite holiness, righteousness, moral and spiritual life," but we are finite "in our organs of life." This limitation "is natural or physical, not spiritual." We can only completely know the "infinite holiness, righteousness, moral and spiritual life" when we no longer are limited by the finiteness of our mortality, "the nature in which we cannot but sin." By sharing in Jesus' death we overcome this finiteness and propensity to sin. Jesus' death was his "supreme act," by which humanity in him "wholly became its whole self" by "wholly ceasing of itself to be all that would limit or contradict itself, and fulfilling all that fulfils and constitutes itself."[68]

Participating in Jesus' death is "something we must do." This shared death is "the death of the nature in which we cannot but sin, and of ourselves who cannot but sin in it." The life we come to know in sharing Christ's death is the meaning of our own death. To illustrate this truth, DuBose recalls Christ's image of the seed that dies and bears much fruit. He notes that it is "legitimate" to understand "the meaning and truth of the death of the seed" in the "much fruit it bears."[69]

Our salvation, our victory over sin, must be "a joint act or activity" of God and ourselves. Our obedience is "not God's but ours." Yet "it is God Himself in us, enabling us to be ourselves and to render to Him what is ours."[70] This clearly points to our transformation as we participate in the saving process. "There is but one truth of the being in Christ, but there are stages or degrees in the realization or actualization of that truth."[71] This progressive transformation is no mere imputation that remains external to us.

DuBose explicitly contradicts an understanding of humanity in Christ as *"simul justus et peccator,"* "at once justified and a sinner," that would allow for no personal advance in holiness through participation in the saving process. He pointedly disagrees with the assumption "that our relation to the so-called saving acts of Christ is wholly an external one," so that they "are in no sense our acts but only acts performed *for* us, in which our sole part is to believe and accept."[72] For DuBose, we are actually and personally transformed in Christ as we participate in the process of salvation: "no man is in any real sense taken up into God who has not in the process wholly taken God into himself."[73] He emphasizes that "to separate too widely the 'done for us' or the 'done instead of our doing' from the 'done with and in and through and by us' and so the '*our* doing too'—has been the source of no little weakness and failure in our current Christianity."[74]

DuBose's understanding of the saving process may be contrasted with Martin Luther's, who states that in justification we are clothed by an "alien righteousness" so that our status before God—but not our nature or personal righteousness—is changed.[75] In contrast, DuBose acknowledges that although God comes to us *as we are*—in our unrighteousness—by divine initiative, our sharing in the divine life does not leave us quite *as we were*. We are meant for personal righteousness in spite of our initial unrighteousness: ". . . if we are in God without righteousness, it is only that we may be in Him for righteousness: our emptiness is for our fulness. Justification by faith as expressive of a present or initial status is only a way to the true end of actual righteousness through faith."[76] He adds that "we are in God for righteousness and life; but that can never be unless we are first taken into God without righteousness and life."[77]

DuBose upholds a personal transformation that begins and continues as we participate in the process of salvation. Our "present peace through faith" is "only the foretaste and beginning of the real peace which we shall enjoy when we are no longer sinners." However, our present peace "*is* a foretaste and a beginning."[78] For DuBose, the righteousness that saves us cannot be "alien" to us. He states, "If Christ's righteousness is never our righteousness it can do us no good; if Christ's death is not actually our death too in Him, we can know nothing of Christ's life as our own."[79] The loss of "faith in an objective real life and salvation" that DuBose perceived in his day was the result of "a practical divorce between the truths of an objective salvation in Christ and a subjective salvation in ourselves." Part of the problem was that the "substitution of the righteousness instead of our own, displaced the need of the righteousness of our own."[80] Our salvation—our holiness, righteousness, and life—must be in Christ and in us.

DuBose likewise states that there is "no such thing" as a grace for us which is not also a grace in us. God "works in us to will and to do in the matter of our salvation not in mere co-operation but only in actual identity with our own working out every jot and tittle of our own salvation, through His grace working not merely with but in us."[81] God is active *in* us and *with* us for our salvation; although salvation in Christ is certainly objective and extrinsic to us, it is to become intrinsic and realized *in* our lives.

DuBose also notes that our being included by participation in Jesus' victory may be contrasted with earthly conquest that is exclusive of others. He explains, "There can be, at the same time, but one Alexander who conquers the world. If there were two, neither would be conqueror of the world. The work of Jesus Christ is the only one which, so far from being exclusive, is inclusive of all men's work. In Him we are potentially, and may be actually, *all*, in the truest and most real sense, conquerors of the world."[82] Jesus is not to be the one and only conqueror of sin and death. We are to be included in his victory as we share in his life by participating in salvation.

Our Free Cooperation with Christ's Salvation

Our "susceptibility" for the divine is the starting point for participation in the saving process whereby the objective gift of salvation in Christ is subjectively realized in us. The one who is "most in the mind of the Gospel of Jesus Christ" is the one who is "most conscious of all the infinite that he is not in himself." Therefore our "insufficiency is our greatness, our poverty is our wealth, our dependence is our glory." Our openness or susceptibility for the divine leads to repentance that is deeper than the "renunciation of sin or of sinful works." Repentance "is the felt and known experience of the fact that in ourselves or in the flesh we are dead as regards the life of the spirit, simply for the fact that the life of the spirit comes not from ourselves or our flesh but from God."[83] This sense of limitation in the human self is fundamental for the needed susceptibility and openness to God.

DuBose also discusses our openness to God in terms of our awareness of sin and the law. The awakening of our consciousness of sin "was the most immediate precondition of the sense of need and the possibility of reception of the grace of holiness."[84] He writes that the "heart of man is the house of God, but God dwells and can dwell only in the contrite heart."[85] Similarly, he notes in *The Gospel According to Saint Paul* that the law exists "to create a need, a capacity, a hunger and thirst for holiness, righteousness, life—so deep, so high, so great, that only God Himself can fill and satisfy it."[86]

It is by faith that our need of God can be fulfilled. DuBose notes, "The principle of holiness is faith, which is that human correspondence with and susceptibility of the divine through which we become partakers of the divine spirit and nature." Our "susceptibility of the divine" is an important element in our participation in the process of salvation, since "there is no limit to what we have in Christ but our own inability to believe and receive."[87]

Conversely, our lack of faith is the limiting factor in "what God is to us in Christ."[88] DuBose urges that "heaven is with us when our eyes are open to see it."[89] In the saving process, "our part, however secondary and subordinate to the divine part, is nevertheless the determining factor."[90] The "length and inefficiency" of the saving process is not due to God's limitation but to ours. "God cannot become Himself-in-us in a moment, only because we are so infinitely incapable of becoming ourselves-in-Him, of being what He is, in a moment."[91] Our freedom gives us the opportunity to reject the saving process. DuBose warns, "While we have no positive power of obedience save as He is and acts in us; yet we have the negative power of non-obedience, *i.e.* of not being and acting in Him. So that even God cannot save us, or be our obedience and righteousness, without us. . . ."[92] Faith is a gift from God, "yet the use and quality or degree of it cannot but rest with us, who are most uncertain quantities."[93] Our faith—or lack of it—is certainly the limiting factor in the saving process.

Our susceptibility for the divine makes possible our saving participation in Christ. But we need more than susceptibility to participate in the process of our own salvation. We must give ourselves freely. We must cooperate. Our *attitude* means everything. Nothing stands between us and all that God is "but our acceptance and appropriation."[94]

Relative to the parable of the Pharisee and the publican, DuBose notes that what Jesus "recognizes in the Publican is the very principle and condition of all human righteousness, knowledge of sin, or repentance, and dependence upon God, or faith."[95] Relative to the parable of the prodigal son, he notes that God "waits to receive us back into full fellowship with Himself and to make our sins as though they had never been," but "even He can go no further unless there be in us the will and the purpose to arise and come to Him."[96] The "types most acceptable" to Jesus "are those whose language is 'God, be merciful to me a sinner!' and 'Father, I have sinned against heaven and before thee, and am not worthy to be called thy son.'"[97] DuBose underscores the importance of *our* attitude in the saving process.

Our right attitude can likewise be expressed in terms of our turning to God and away from self. DuBose notes that we are "sinners insomuch and so long as we seek ourselves and not God, or until we find our life in Him and not in ourselves." Accordingly, faith is "that attitude and disposition towards God which, carried to its limit or made perfect, is oneness with Himself and participation in His holiness, righteousness, and life; and which as such is resurrection from the sin and death to which we are subject in ourselves alone."[98]

Our attitude toward sin and our attitude toward holiness are essentially one attitude. DuBose notes that "there can be no hatred of sin that is not a positive and definite love of holiness."[99] He thus resolves the whole Christian life into the question of attitude toward sin. With respect to the term "sin," he urges, "that one word covers all that will impede, contradict, impair, or destroy life or that constitutes death."[100] Recalling the prodigal son's awareness of both his sins and his identity as a sinner, he states that "everything depends upon man's own attitude towards sin and his own sin." This attitude "we express by the word *repentance*"; that is, the only right attitude towards sin is repentance, "whose end is the putting away of sin," and the only right attitude towards holiness or God is faith, "whose promise and fulfilment is the 'God in us and we in God' of Jesus Christ."[101]

God's impartation of righteousness follows our repentance. DuBose explains, "Upon repentance from sin and faith in God, God sees and receives the sinner in Christ. He no longer reckons or imputes to him the sin which he himself repudiates and disowns, but invests him with, as his own, the holiness or righteousness which he sees and appropriates to himself by faith in Christ."[102] Repentance is thus at the heart of the saving process. "Repentance is nothing else than that attitude towards sin which, when carried to its limit or made complete, is the death to it which Jesus Christ Himself died."[103]

DuBose warns against "two opposite misinterpretations" that concern our participation in the process of salvation. On the one hand, there is the misinterpretation that misses the reality and actuality of "the ever *present* power and fact" of Christ's death and resurrection in us, "supposing that Christ is in us merely by influence, or effect or resemblance."[104] This view would advocate a kind of salvation in Christ "by sample" or mere example. DuBose sharply opposes this misinterpretation because the power of Christ's presence was such a vivid reality for him. Although Christ's life was exemplary, Christ was no mere sample for salvation.

On the other hand, DuBose also contradicts any view of the saving process that would call for human personality to be displaced, overwhelmed, or annihilated by Christ's presence. He notes, "the other misapprehension is that of so conceiving of St. Paul's 'not I, but Christ in me' as to practically do away with our own personality."[105] He urges in *High Priesthood and Sacrifice* that "if God without us should make our wills His own, it would not be our wills that He had made His own." Instead, God "has made us rational and free" and "has endowed us with a personality whose essence consists in our own self-accomplishment and becoming." God will not violate "by one jot or tittle our personal constitution or our spiritual task or business."[106] God does not displace our freedom or human personality to save us.

God invites us, and—if we will—God indwells us, shares life with us and saves us. But God does not *force* us to be saved. DuBose states that

"God's being and acting in us is consistent with, and in no sense or degree contradictory or destructive of, our own personal being or acting."[107] The saving process calls for the fulfillment of divinity in humanity and of humanity in divinity through our freely chosen participation in the gift of salvation in Christ.

Love and Mutuality in Our Saving Relationship with Christ

DuBose emphasizes that our participation in the saving process must lead to a mutuality of giving in personal relationship whereby Christ lives in us and we live in Christ. The saving process is two-sided, not one-sided. God is to be fulfilled in humanity, and humanity is to be fulfilled in God. This unitive mutual fulfilment does not obliterate the distinctness of Christ's personality or ours. The one who participates in the saving process "can be only freely free," engaging "the freedom of himself, of his own will and his whole self." It is this freedom that makes true mutuality possible in the divine-human relationship. For the one who participates in the saving process, DuBose urges, "it must be himself fulfilling God's will as well as God's will fulfilling itself in him."[108]

DuBose suggests marriage as an analogy for this distinctness-in-unity: "the ideal of the union of husband and wife is not that one should become a nonentity; but that both should retain their personalities in a perfectly free union of minds, wills, and lives." Our saving union with Christ also involves a free union of our minds, wills, and lives as we participate in the process of salvation. This analogy of marriage can be understood more fully in light of God's realization of himself as love. DuBose states that "God might have manifested himself as goodness in a merely immanental relation to the universe of which there was no consciousness in the latter; but He could only manifest Himself as love through a transcendental and personal relation to beings who could know Him as such and love Him in return."[109]

Love calls for mutuality in giving, which in turn calls for free, conscious personalities who choose to give to one another. Love cannot be forced or manipulated. It is not inevitable. Our participation in love involves our freely giving of ourselves, and sharing in a mutuality of affection. Christ's love in us makes possible our own love, our life in God, and our victory over death. DuBose explains that "nothing less than love—divine love, that love which is God Himself in us—will consume and destroy the self of the flesh, and quicken and kindle the spirit of God and of life in us."[110] He urges that "it is not the being loved but the loving with a divine love that is our salvation."[111] Our giving in love is our truest receiving of the love that saves us in a saving process that is deeply relational, engaging our lives with Christ and with each other in his name.

DuBose emphasizes the *personal* character of love in our saving relationship with Christ. We receive our human nature without our own choosing, but our life in Christ involves a personal relationship of love in response to the personal love that Christ offers us. He states, "Our relation to Adam is a natural one; our relation to Christ is a personal one. We are one with Adam by fact of our nature; we are one with Christ only by act of our persons or of ourselves."[112] The personal nature of this saving divine-human relationship reflects both who God is and who we are. There is a real and free mutuality in the relationship we share with God. This relationship is not "necessary," in the sense that our humanity is simply a given which we passively inherit. Instead, our saving relationship with God "has to be personally entered into, and only exists where it has been personally entered into from both sides."[113]

As we participate in God's love, we share it generously. For DuBose, there is an essential unity of love and giving. He notes in *The Reason of Life* that human life, "as the life of God, is essentially and necessarily a ministry and a service. It lives in giving itself, and ceases to live in ceasing to give."[114] Love is "the only real and perfect bond or principle of union and unity." Therefore "God is Love, and all life is love." Only in doing God's "work of love are we sharing His life of love, and enjoying the blessedness of it." With us and with God, life and blessedness are found in giving rather than in receiving. He notes that "there is no either true giving of self, or true self or life to give, that is not Love."[115]

THE END OR GOAL OF THE SAVING PROCESS: ARISTOTLE, EVOLUTION, AND DISCONTINUITY

DuBose explains the saving process, especially the end and completion of the saving process, in terms of an ancient teleology and a very contemporary biology. He draws upon Aristotle's understanding of the meaning of all things in terms of their intended and potential end, and the scientific theory of evolution which prompted enormous controversy in his day. Together these concepts describe the end and completion of the saving process.

Aristotle and Our Human Meaning

Aristotle was a major influence on DuBose, who recalled that it was early in his teaching career that he began to use Aristotle's *Ethics* "for both the Greek and the philosophy." He discovered that "unconsciously Aristotle became the basis and starting point of all my thinking." DuBose's ethics course in the university was a requirement for all members of the new theological class after theological instruction resumed around 1880 at Sewanee. In this course DuBose sought to draw out "the unity and continuity of the Ethics and the Exegesis," and to establish that "from Aristotle to Christ was a well-travelled course."[116] After retirement, from 1913 to 1918 DuBose began to write out his class lectures for publication as part of a larger work, "From Aristotle to Christ." However, this work was not completed at the time of his death.[117]

For Aristotle as for DuBose, "Nothing can be fully known save in the light of its *end*." DuBose concludes that Aristotle is defined by his statement, "What a thing is when its becoming has been completed, that we call the nature of the thing, as *e.g.* of man."[118] Similarly, DuBose states that the meaning and definition of a thing is to be found in the completion of what it is to *become*.[119] He claims Aristotle as authority for the principle that "everything is to be defined by its end, by what it will be when its becoming is completed and it is perfect."[120] "The good of any being, says Aristotle substantially, is that which completes its nature, and perfects its functions—brings all its potentialities into actuality."[121] He adds that "the true nature and law of things are what they are coming to, and not what they already are."[122] DuBose applies this principle in his definition of humanity. He states that "to know what we are, we need to know all that we shall be." Our salvation must therefore fulfil our "ideal," our "conception," the "what it were to be it" of humanity.[123] He urges that "all processes are best read and understood in their highest reaches: it is the end that interprets and explains all things."[124]

DuBose holds that "the truth of any form of life, even a plant, is not whatever it happens to be, but what it ought to be, and must be, in order to be itself."[125] As an example he develops the analogy of an acorn which is really understood only in terms of its "destination" to become an oak tree. All acorns do not in fact *become* oaks "because there lie many conditions and many hindrances between; but every acorn has an inherent impulse and disposition to be an oak."[126] Accordingly, all acorns are to be understood in terms of their destiny to become oak trees, whether or not their destiny becomes a reality in individual cases. We all have "the nature and the natural destiny" to become sons or daughters of God, but this does not "become so by a mere immanent process of natural evolution" or "the operation of laws and forces wholly within" ourselves; our destiny is realized "in reaction and cooperation with agents outside" ourselves.[127]

DuBose's teleology may be compared with Thomas Aquinas' under-standing of God as the final cause and ultimate end. Both DuBose and Aquinas drew on Aristotle in their presentations of Christian theology. Aquinas holds that God is "the productive cause of all things" and "the end of all things."[128] "The ultimate end of things is to become like God."[129] "Each thing intends, as its ultimate end, to be united with God as closely as is possible for it."[130] Accordingly, "the ultimate end of man, and of every intellectual substance, is called felicity or happiness," and "the ultimate happiness and felicity of every intellectual substance is to know God."[131] No creature can constitute human happiness.[132] The perfection and per-fect happiness of the human intellect is "through union with God," in which "alone man's happiness consists."[133] This happiness may also be termed beatitude or the beatific vision. Aquinas parallels DuBose's view of human at-one-ment with God as the intended end, fulfilment, and mean-ing of our life.

The end and destination of all things, humanity included, leads to a persistence and restlessness until that end is realized because the real end "can never cease acting as an end." It "is the end that determines the whole nature and process, the whole life and destiny, of every being in the universe." Accordingly, it is not enough to say that the acorn can only be understood in terms of its destination as an oak tree. It is also necessary to say that the "acorn can never rest until it is an oak." In this sense, the completion and "rest" of humanity "is the rest of God." Nothing less will do. Our hearts are restless until they rest in God. DuBose urges that "no finite or temporal meaning and reason and end" of humanity will ever satisfy the "craving" for "more life, all life, the life of God." Humanity "will not stop short of its true conception, and can never be content to stop short of its actual attainment in Jesus Christ," in whom "we rest in the perfected and satisfied sense of accomplished relationship or oneness with God."[134]

DuBose describes the accomplished relationship or oneness with God in explicitly filial terms, as revealed for us in Jesus' completed sonship.[135] Jesus "saved humanity by making it, first in Him and then in itself, son of God; thus raising it out of itself and sin and death into God and holi-ness and life." Our destiny is filial because humanity is by nature consti-tuted "*to become* son of God." Accordingly, Jesus Christ is the "end or completion, and so predestination, of humanity."[136] In Jesus, our human "destination" is a personal, relational and saving union with God. DuBose explains that since God is love, all things from the beginning "mean, and are destined to come to, love in the end."[137] Our human end,

completion, and rest—and therefore our human definition and meaning—are found in loving relationship with God.

The completed relationship of at-one-ment with God is our salvation
from sin and death. Simply stated, "there is no other Salvation for disunion
from God but union with God." This union, or "At-one-ment" with God,
expresses "the great truth that in Jesus Christ we have been made *at one*, and
one, with God." DuBose urges that our completion in this saving process is
really a matter of life or death: "In proportion, therefore, as God is in us and
we in Him, we spiritually *live:* in proportion as we are not in Him or He in
us, we are, by no mere figure but in very fact, spiritually *dead.*"[138] In terms of
the teleology of Aristotle, our intended end is union with God. Our "destination" is to be saved from separation from God. At-one-ment with God is
our completion and our definition as human beings.

Victor Lyle Dowdell quotes Walter H. Moberly's statement that
DuBose "never tired of insisting upon the necessity of the Aristotelian principle of explanation through the end."[139] Dowdell concludes that DuBose's
"intellectual profundity is unquestionably due to his absorption of Aristotle." Dowdell also finds that "the stamp of DuBose's great mind still appears
in young clergymen who have been nurtured in the University of the South;
thus the influence of Aristotle on the American Episcopal Church is greater
than might have been expected."[140]

Evolution and the Completion of the Saving Process

DuBose received the theory of evolution gladly, and incorporated it into his
soteriology. He focused his theology "on the idea that the universe was in a
continual process of evolution and movement toward God."[141] He notes that
the "unity of the natural and the spiritual, that matter exists for mind, necessity for freedom, the earth for man, and finally man for Christ as Christ for
God" is "all from beginning to end a drama of evolution as scientific as it is
rational and religious." He also observes that "it may be too much to say that
Christianity anticipates the modern teaching of evolution, but that teaching
certainly wonderfully adapts itself to the expression of Christianity."[142]

Although DuBose affirms evolutionary theory as a way to understand
and express truth about Christian faith, he also points very distinctly beyond
evolutionary theory as an ultimate explanation for the meaning of life. He
states, "The evolution or transition from necessary to free, from physical to
spiritual, from product of nature to child of God, will never be scientifically
traceable or explicable. Life has depths of mystery in it far beneath the
plummet of any earthly student of mere phenomena."[143] He embraces the

truths of scientific investigation and their implications for theology, but he clearly recognizes that the ultimate source of those truths is beyond scientific analysis or quantification.

DuBose states that the "natural end" is not "the final cause for which God creates. The end of the natural is but the starting-point of the spiritual."[144] Our destination is to "something more than natural relation to God."[145] He adds that "the end to which all things have worked has been the production of the natural man; and that the end to which all things are working is the production of the spiritual man."[146] He explains that "the whole natural order of which man is the head, in what we call Adam, was predestined and is destined to be taken up and included in the higher spiritual order of which man is still the head in Christ."[147]

DuBose saw the end of spiritual evolution and the whole evolutionary process in the saving at-one-ment of humanity and God. Because the evolutionary process points beyond humanity's headship over natural creation, the fulfilment of anthropology is therefore christological. "Man as he is, Adam, has been the goal of the natural creation—man as he is to be, Christ, is the goal of the spiritual creation."[148] The Incarnation is thus "the truth of truths, the end of ends," and "the self-realization of God in his creation, of the whole creation in God."[149] Christ is the fulfilment of creation, and evolution, and even of divinity. DuBose finds that "there is a propriety in viewing and designating Creation as a whole as Son of God, inasmuch as it is all One, and, as it came from, so it is destined to return to Him in the final inheritance of sonship." He likewise states, "when it is said (Eph. i. 5) that 'God foreordained, or predestinated, us unto the adoption as sons unto Himself through Jesus Christ,' it means that the life which came to us from God as our father is ultimately to return to Him in our own realized and accomplished sonship." Jesus is thus at the pivot point of creation's fulfilment in return to God. "Creation, in man as its head, was through the world-movement of evolution to return to its Source and at-one itself with God in the person of the God-man."[150]

The teleology of Aristotle and evolutionary theory are both evident in DuBose's soteriology. The meaning of our life is Christ, just as union with Christ is our destination and our salvation. The end of the evolutionary process is likewise Christ, just as union with Christ is the destination and completion of all creation. DuBose states that "the Christ of the future is the goal and crown of the entire creation of God."[151] There is more to the evolutionary process than the development of humanity as the highest part of nature because the end and zenith of the evolutionary process is Christ.

This process will be fulfilled when humanity and all creation are one in the encosmic Christ. In this regard, DuBose anticipates Pierre Teilhard de Chardin, who sees Christ to be "Christ-Omega" and "the evolver" who "animates and gathers up all the biological and spiritual energies developed by the universe."[152]

DuBose also understands the saving process in terms of all life's return to the Creator in the destined fulfilment of at-one-ing relationship. He describes life and creation in terms of a process that flows from God and ultimately is to return to God: "the life which in the end comes to itself in God, in the beginning came from Itself in God."[153] DuBose's approach may also be compared to Thomas Aquinas' understanding of the "*exitus et reditus*" (emergence and return) of all things "according to the pattern of their proceeding from God as their source . . . and insofar as they return to him as their end."[154]

God is the source from whom all life has come into being, and the source of all life and evolutionary processes. DuBose urges that "all evolution is the coming of Life: it is the divine process by which the Transcendent becomes immanent—the Eternal in the temporal, the Infinite in the finite, the Perfect in the imperfect, God in the world."[155] Relative to the prologue of the Gospel according to John, he writes, "When he says, 'In Him (the Logos) was life,' the principal truth I find in the words, or underlying the words, is this: Life did not originate as one of the changes, accidents, or effects in evolution, but existed before and was the subject of evolution."[156] He upholds "the truth that life, like reason, is not merely the end and product of the cosmic process we call evolution, but was also its antecedent principle, its formal and formative cause, its substance and subject."[157] DuBose finds in the creation an expression of the process by which all life comes from God, and is to return to God and have its meaning in God: "The material universe is a concrete expression of an ideal principle, which not only as first-cause gives it existence, but as final-cause gives it reason, meaning, and purpose. Indeed Final Cause or Purpose is the only first-cause or ultimate real cause at all: through it, and it alone, all things come into being and have their being."[158] In this regard, he is consistent with his teleological emphasis on understanding the meaning of things relative to their end. The final cause of at-one-ment of all with God is the fulfilment of return to God which also completes the first cause and movement from God that is the creation of all. He explains that "final cause and sufficient reason reveal themselves only in the consummation and completion of processes and evolutions."[159] At-one-ment with God is the end and meaning of creation, evolution, and the process of salvation.

In light of both teleology and evolution, we can understand ourselves as participants in a process that is already and objectively completed in Christ. He notes that "Jesus Christ is the truth to us of our spiritual, God-related, divine manhood, our predestined sonship to God. As humanity psychically or naturally culminated in Adam, or man as he is in himself or in nature, so humanity will spiritually culminate in Christ, or man as he will be in God."[160] Christ was thus "the end of an evolutional process." Christ "was the End and Heir of the world, inasmuch as He was its reason revealed, its meaning interpreted, its purpose accomplished."[161] DuBose states, "Jesus Christ as man has attained, represents, and *is* the spiritual, moral, and natural end or destination, the *rest*, of humanity. In faith we *have* attained it in Him, and through faith we *shall* attain it in Him."[162] This process is not yet completed, but it is to be subjectively realized in us as we come to be at-one with our Lord who is "the goal and crown of the entire creation of God."[163]

Discontinuity in the Process of Salvation

Although DuBose has at times been identified as a "process theologian," or as a forerunner of process theology, he explicitly disavows any understanding of process or change within the divine life during the process of human salvation. He notes that "God in Himself is complete without process, but God in the world is completed only in process, by evolution, and the end of that process or evolution is Jesus Christ, in Whom God and the world and man are One."[164] Although salvation and evolution are to be completed in a processive way, he certainly does not perceive God to be subordinate to a universal creative process. Speaking of "a newer and truer construction of Christianity today," DuBose states that "the New of God is always the Old: the newness is in us, not in Him or in It."[165] For DuBose, there is no immanental process of divine change or evolution, although God is involved in creation's process of evolution and change that will culminate in the atonement of all in Christ. The change and evolution of the saving process concern our relationship with God, not God's inner life. "There is no real change in God into what He was not before in Himself, but there was a relative change in what He was to the other parties through change in them in their relation to Him."[166] DuBose is no "process theologian."

Furthermore, the process by which the objective in Christ may become subjectively realized in us is much more than a gradual evolution from good to better to best. The process of salvation requires a distinct and sharp discontinuity between the human beginning condition and the end of the process in at-one-ment with God. This discontinuity concerns our state of separation from God from which we need to be *saved.*

For DuBose, "salvation does not mean a normal transition or translation from a lower into a higher good, but a deliverance from an *evil* into a good."[167] He emphasizes that the very notion of salvation implies salvation *from* something. Salvation is ever so much more than a mere process of improvement, or the inevitable continuation of divine creativity; our "salvation from sin to holiness, from death to life" was won for us at the cost of Jesus' life.[168] In this way, DuBose squarely faces the reality of human sin and its consequences. He states, "As oneness with God is holiness, so a spiritual and personal separation and difference from God is *sin.* Sin is what we are when God is *not* in us. . . . If then holiness is the divine nature, sin is a nature or a condition of nature in us not of God and not divine. It is the negation or contradiction of holiness. Disunion, separation, enmity with God is thus an actual state of things."[169] Accordingly, he explains, our only possible reunion with God "is the removal of that which separates."[170] Sin separates us from God and must be removed.

Discontinuity is necessarily involved in the removal of what separates us from God. DuBose urges, "Our life in God is no simple, natural, and painless birth out of the natural into the spiritual, out of ourselves *not yet* in God into ourselves *in* God; it is a life out of ourselves in separation from, and at enmity, with God into ourselves at one, in union and unity, with God."[171] DuBose emphasizes this discontinuity in dramatic and anthropomorphic terms, urging that there is "a war within us unto death," and that either the "man of the flesh" or the "man of the spirit" must die in each of us.

Indeed, DuBose is so emphatic about sin that his theology of salvation is at times "sin-centered" in focus. In *High Priesthood and Sacrifice* he defines the meaning and way of holiness in terms of our meeting and overcoming sin "in our environment and in ourselves." He likewise identifies sin as "the one thing that stands in our way, between us and ourselves, between us and everything else, between us and God."[172]

It is this discontinuity concerning the human need for salvation from sin and separation from God that distinguishes DuBose from the process theologians. For example, his treatment of human sin and our need for salvation can be sharply contrasted with the approach of Norman Pittenger, a twentieth-century Anglican process theologian. In his book *Alfred North Whitehead*, Pittenger states, "In the creative process he [God] has permitted radical freedom, so that evil is a possibility, and among men sinful decision can (and does) lead to tragic situations. Yet God's love is faithful and inexhaustible; it is able to 'take' this evil and sin, to absorb what is bad and to use what is good. In spite of evil and sin, good can emerge through the patient, tender, never-failing 'overruling' of God as he provides for and 'governs' his world in love."[173] Pittenger does not draw out the connection of human evil and sin with separation from God. Instead of our needing salvation from sin and separation, our sin is "absorbed" into God. For Pittenger, there does not seem to be a real discontinuity in the saving process because there is no real separation from God.

Pittenger understands human sin in terms of frustrated or imperfect love, without taking into account the reality of separation from God. He explains,

> Man is a dynamic creature, moving towards fulfilment yet free to decide against this fulfilment.... But his true achievement or self-real-ization is only as he loves. In God's intention he is such a lover, yet he is frustrated in his loving, and in consequence of wrong decisions he may and does distort that which is deepest in him. Thus he is a "sin-ner"; he needs what we might style "re-alignment" with the divine intention for him. His sinning is not so much disobedience to some moral code, some set of commandments, or some imposed law; it is a violation of his loving relationship with God and his fellows and hence a violation of his own drive towards love.[174]

In contrast, DuBose clearly understands the removal of what separates us from God in terms of a discontinuity that is neither simple, natural, nor easy. He explains, "the sinlessness or holiness of Jesus could no more than ours be a painless experience."[175] The overcoming of sin is no mere "realign-ment," as described by Pittenger. DuBose states in *The Gospel in the Gospels*, "faith comes only through trial. The highest and latest energy and act of our personality, that by which we conquer the world and transcend earthly lim-itations and conditions, is not attained easily and painlessly."[176] He under-stands St. Paul to uphold the position that "all real good, natural or spiritual, is won against, is a victory over, an opposite ill." Virtue is likewise "the very product or fruit of conflict with and conquest of its opposite."[177] Faith is "perfected by the things it suffers and survives."[178] Accordingly, holiness can exist for us only by "resisting and overcoming" sin.[179] DuBose's understand-ing of discontinuity in the saving process is distinguishable from Pittenger's. The discontinuity of breaking from sin is at the heart of the saving process for DuBose.

Jesus' condemnation was not for sinners, but for those who do not know themselves to be sinners, and "who will not to be, and will not be, saved from their sin."[180] DuBose understood the knowledge of sin to be "the beginning of holiness," and he understood the conquest of sin to be "for us the only way, if not the very truth and life, of holiness."[181] Divine salvation is the only deliverance from sin, and "humanity can be or become itself only through a redemption or salvation from sin and the death which is its consequence."[182] For DuBose, the saving process must include the discontinuity of salvation from our sins and the separation from God that accompanies sin.

DuBose's system of theology is fundamentally a soteriology. He emphasizes the reality of the saving process by which Jesus' life/death/resurrection experience may be actualized in our own lives. The completion of this process is the intended end, fulfilment, and meaning of our humanity. Through participation in this process we are saved *from* our sins and separation from God. The destined end and meaning of our lives are realized as we come to be at-one with God, and as all creation returns to God in Christ. The objective reality of Christ's offer of salvation is to be subjectively realized in us. Even though we have not yet completed the saving process or fully realized the objective gift of salvation, this saving gift is already true for us in Christ. It will be increasingly a reality *in us* as we participate in the saving process.

William Porcher DuBose as a cadet at The Citadel
Courtesy of the Archive, The University of the South, Sewanee, Tennessee

A holograph of
DuBose's writing
Courtesy of the Archive,
The University of the
South, Sewanee, Tennessee

DuBose in academic gown
Courtesy of the Archive, The University of the South, Sewanee, Tennessee

DuBose receiving a token of appreciation at the reunion with his former students, August 1911, Sewanee, Tennessee

Courtesy of the Archive, The University of the South, Sewanee, Tennessee

CHAPTER 3

The Christ

DuBose upholds the fullness of divinity and humanity in the Incarnation, but he finds that Jesus' humanity has been slighted in much of Christian theology. A distinctive feature of DuBose's christology is the role of human freedom in the Incarnation: Jesus had freedom to choose between obedience and disobedience. Recognizing his human limitation, turning from self to God, Jesus experienced the same process that is to be our way of salvation. This was for Jesus the way of the cross, a way of loving sacrifice and generosity that we may share. DuBose's "spirit christology" is another distinctive feature of his christology. By the Spirit, Jesus received divine assistance to live a human life that was righteous, holy, and without sin. He lived and completed the way of salvation by grace through faith. Jesus embodies and reveals the fulfilment of at-one-ment with God that is the end, destiny, and meaning of our lives.

DuBose's christology was preeminently a christology of salvation. DuBose states, "there is no task or function of Incarnation but human redemption and salvation."[1] His christology also sought to counter what he saw as an exaggerated emphasis on Jesus' divinity at the expense of his humanity. While firmly upholding the divinity of Christ, he also emphasized that Jesus humanly reveals the way of our salvation. DuBose's emphasis on recovering appreciation for Jesus' full humanity is also consistent with his methodological focus on the role of human experience in the saving process. Jesus' deity was "infinitely true," but "it was humanly manifested, and cannot be known or expressed by us otherwise than in what He was as man."[2] Jesus' divinity was revealed through his human experience, and it is through his human experience that we are to know salvation. Jesus humanly lives the saving process through perfect faith and obedience. In his life, death, and resurrection he reveals the end of the process of salvation in which God and humanity are at one and the "veil of separation" between God and humanity is removed. Jesus humanly reveals how we are to be included in the Incarnation, and share fully in the saving benefits of his victory over sin and death.

DuBose's christology has been a subject of misunderstanding and controversy. He upholds Jesus' full humanity in radical and even startling terms, which has led some to question his orthodoxy. Such criticisms were present during DuBose's time, and they still appear today. Francis J. Hall, another theologian in the Episcopal Church of the late nineteenth and early twentieth centuries, states in a book review that DuBose "begins with the human aspects of the Gospel, and, we think, yields to the current tendency to emphasize that aspect out of due proportion." Hall urges that "in starting at the human end," DuBose "has deprived his readers in much of his treatise of the interpretive principle—our Lord's divine Person—which enables His Manhood to be understood."[3]

Criticism of DuBose's christology continued after his death. In 1925, a reviewer of J. O. F. Murray's *DuBose as a Prophet of Unity* warned that "the danger of the Nestorian heresy is so ever menacing in a humanitarian age like the present that all language which seems to imply that the Lord of Glory was not only Man but a man, an individual Jew, is greatly to be deprecated."[4] Similarly, in 1989, John Pearce concluded his review of Alexander's anthology of DuBose's work with the statement, "of course it has sometimes been true that we have overemphasized the divinity of Christ at the expense of his humanity, but it may be that DuBose has fallen into the opposite trap."[5] In light of such criticisms, this study will present both the traditional and innovative aspects of DuBose's christology and demonstrate that his understanding of the Christ is consistently orthodox.

THE FULL HUMANITY OF JESUS CHRIST

Jesus' Human Personality and Nature

At the heart of DuBose's christology was his insistent upholding of the full humanity of Jesus Christ. He notes that "it in no wise conflicts with the eternal essential Sonship of our Incarnate Lord, to say that as man He was subject to the universal human law and process of becoming son of God."[6] Jesus' resurrection was, "as ours must be, on its human side an act of faith in God, as on the divine side it was an operation of the power of God, or of grace, in humanity."[7] Jesus humanly lived the saving process to completion in the same way that we are to share.

DuBose upheld the fullness of humanity and divinity in the Incarnation, although he perceived that Christian theology had often tended to affirm the divinity at the expense of Jesus' humanity. These understandings of the Christ can be characterized as Docetic, Apollinarian or Monophysite in tendency. DuBose notes that "partial, defective views of his human activities, knowledge and power,—a higher or psychical Docetism,—characterize our current theology."[8] Similarly, he advises that "the constant disposition and effort to make our Lord more divine by making him less human tends only to reduce the incarnation to a semblance and an unreality."[9] The christological perspective that DuBose resisted is epitomized by Everhard Digges La Touche, who "argued that the notion that in the Incarnation Christ took up and had to fight against the sinful heritage of humanity within Himself was 'repulsive' and struck 'at the very roots of the reality of the Incarnation.'"[10] Such a christology would not recognize Jesus' human struggle for obedience in the fully human nature that we share (including its weaknesses). Luker notes that DuBose was directly attacked by Everhard Digges La Touche "at precisely this point."[11] In contrast, DuBose holds that Jesus' humanity was identical to our own and his human life was identical to our own—except that his faith was perfect and he was personally sinless.

For DuBose, more is less when an overemphasis on the divinity serves to marginalize the humanity of Jesus in our understanding. He advises that "the constant disposition and effort to make our Lord more divine by making him less human tends only to reduce the incarnation to a semblance and an unreality."[12] DuBose notes the "disposition common to us all" to view Jesus' temptations as "experiences that are not human," and to see in Jesus "one who was not truly man,"[13] and he urges that "it is hard for any of us to realize to what extent we ascribe to our Lord the merest impersonal human nature, and make all his *personal* life in it, not human at all, but purely and only divine."[14] For DuBose, Christian theology had often tended to affirm the divinity of Christ at the expense of his humanity, resulting in a christology that was seriously out of balance and distorted.

DuBose points to occasions when the full humanity of Jesus has been slighted in the history of christology, even if unintentionally or with the intent to acknowledge the union of Jesus' humanity and divinity. He warns that "during the conciliar period the divinity of our Lord shone too brightly for all to be able to see and appreciate the completeness in its every detail of his humanity." For example, some fourth-century theologians held the real humanity of Jesus "as a whole." But, DuBose asserts, "they were unconsciously not holding it in all its details or in all the parts that were necessary to the integrity of the whole."[15]

Apollinaris (d. ca. 390), Bishop of Laodicea, "charged that a whole deity and a whole humanity in Christ were two and could by no possibility be one."[16] To this, DuBose responds, "Jesus Christ was God and man, but he was with them, too, so overpoweringly and controllingly God that he was very infinitesimally man. The humanity in the Godhead was as a drop of honey in the ocean."[17] It was "natural" that the age which had upheld Christ's divinity "with such ability and with so much difficulty and suffering" would "unconsciously and unintentionally feel and appreciate less the importance, in its details as well as in its totality, of a scientific analysis and construction of the real humanity." However "natural" or understandable such errors of the fourth century may have been, there was no room for a diminishment of Jesus' humanity in DuBose's theological system. Whatever "the danger of falling into the error of a dual personality, or the difficulty of ascribing to our one Lord the whole activity of God and the whole activity of man," DuBose urges, "we must not get over it by making human salvation any less an act of man in God than an act of God in man."[18]

DuBose's concern about inadequate presentations of Jesus' humanity was also expressed in terms that were consistent with his systematic emphasis on salvation. He considers that the "most serious criticism" of patristic and later christological thought "is that a one-sided view of our Lord's person led to a much more one-sided view of his work." The danger of a "one-sided" christology "in which the human is unduly subordinated to the divine" is that it "leads to a soteriology in which the human part is still more unduly lost in the divine." He also laments that in the "dominant theology," every "distinctive term descriptive of human salvation" is "interpreted almost wholly as an act of God and hardly at all as an act even in man, much less of man."[19] To the extent that Jesus' humanity is crowded out by his divinity, his life is not a human redemption in which the saving process is humanly completed.

DuBose contradicted this "one-sided" tendency, and upheld the fullness of Jesus' human nature in terms of his "personality." He states, "Jesus Christ was not saved by any difference of nature from ours; nor from any difference of actual condition from ours."[20] He notes in the preface to the new edition of *Soteriology*, "Reference has been made to my application of a human personality to our Lord." Then he takes pains to uphold the classical and orthodox position that Christ was "one and the same personal being, or subject," thereby denying the misinterpretation that Christ had "a human personality distinct from His divine personality, in the sense of His being a divine person united with another human person."[21]

Mutual Fulfilment of Divinity and Humanity in Jesus

DuBose upholds "the equal truth of the essential and unique deity, and the completely human divinity of our one Lord."[22] Christ is "as truly God as man, and as truly man as God."[23] Jesus is as much "the divine grace by which we are saved" as "the human faith and obedience through which we are saved. Jesus is both the "*salvatio salvans*," the "divine operating causes," "as well as the human elements, the operated effects, the faith and obedience, the *salvatio salvata*." He is both "God saving" and humanity saved.[24] In him we see the perfection of divine initiative for our salvation and human faithful response for the completion of the saving process.

In Jesus, humanity and divinity were perfectly fulfilled in each other. We may understand this mutual fulfilment in terms of love. Love is fulfilled as it is given and received in mutual sharing. God's love for humanity is perfectly expressed in the Incarnation, as humanity's love for God is perfectly expressed in Jesus' life. The love of divine gift for human salvation and of human faithful response in the saving process are both fulfilled in Jesus.

Jesus likewise represents the fulfilment of God in all creation, and the fulfilment of all creation in God. DuBose explains that "the heir of all things is He in whom all things terminate, have their fulfilment and come to their natural or determined end." Jesus is "not only God in all things, but no less all things in God." By his perfect faith, obedience, and love, Jesus represents the response of creation to the grace of God. In Christ was "God's absolute gift of Himself to the world," and "by His grace in it, the world's supreme gift of itself to God."[25] Although this response is not yet fulfilled and completed in all of creation (as it is not yet fulfilled and completed in all of humanity), it is already represented, fulfilled, and completed in Christ, as it is to be fulfilled in all creation and humanity in and through him.

The Fullness of Jesus' Human Personality

DuBose points to the full range of Jesus' human experience to argue for the fullness of Jesus' human personality and nature, which would have been compromised and unreal if he had lived a "purely God-determined life" that lacked the "distinctive property of self-determination or freedom."[26] Jesus' righteousness was for DuBose a human righteousness—not a divine righteousness enacted by a being that *seemed* human. Jesus was "human through and through, none the less divine for being human, nor less divine in any part than in all."[27] DuBose urges that Jesus' "human consciousness, reason, will, freedom, and activity" which have been acknowledged by the church constitute human personality "in all human thinking and speaking." He subsequently challenged the notion that "the Logos assumed only so much of humanity as is impersonal," and lacked "all that constitutes in us our human personality."[28] The Incarnation did not represent a displacement of human consciousness by divine consciousness, which would belie the reality of Jesus' human nature and personality.

DuBose lived in a time of growing interest in human psychology, personality, and experience, and he explored Jesus' human life, personality, and psychology—especially with reference to Jesus' faith, obedience, and human fulfilment of the saving process. In the Incarnation Christ assumed this fullness of humanity "*as it is.*"[29] Jesus' life "was subject to all the conditions, laws, and processes that belong to human life in general."[30] For DuBose, Jesus' humanity was no different from ours. His life was "utterly" a life of faith, and his faith was a human faith "in all its conditions and manifestations." As Jesus' faith was a human faith, "equally His obedience was a human obedience."[31] Jesus' human holiness, righteousness, and life were no different from our holiness, righteousness, and life are to be in him.

If Jesus' humanity had been somehow "different," the fullness of our humanity would not have been assumed or saved in the Incarnation, and the saving path and process of Jesus' life would have been different from our way of salvation. DuBose notes that "for our Lord to have been spared the least of all He endured and overcame, would have been to abridge by just so much the completeness and perfection of His attainment and exaltation."[32] Indeed, if the Logos were manifested "partly as man and partly as God by the side of or from behind the man," it "might be a Theophany or a Logophany." But such a mixed manifestation would have been "no true and perfect Incarnation."[33] In the Incarnation, Christ fully assumed fallen human nature, including human weakness, susceptibility to temptation and sin, and mortality. Jesus shared with us "all our deficiencies and insufficiencies, all our natural weaknesses and impossibilities."[34] Jesus' humanity was real and uncompromised. He was fully divine, fully human, fully one.

Jesus' Human Weakness and Victory

Jesus experienced the limitations of human nature. Otherwise, to have "imported" into Jesus' human nature "the freedom from limitation of the divine nature would have been to contradict and nullify it." He "experienced to the limit the impotence of the human will," and "uttered the universal experience and voice of humanity when He said, I can of myself do nothing."[35] Jesus' human will was "impotent" in the sense that he was not humanly self-sufficient—as *none* of us is humanly self-sufficient. Jesus lived our path of righteousness and salvation by acknowledging his own human limitation, and receiving the grace of divine assistance from beyond himself in human terms. Instead of relying on himself and his own will, Jesus turned to God in perfect faith and obedience; he taught his disciples to pray that God the Father's "will be done." Faithful to his own teaching, in his agony at Gethsemane he prayed that God the Father's will would be done.

In sharing our human insufficiency relative to salvation, Jesus was the "supreme demonstration and manifestation" that we can only become our true selves by God, "not by nature nor by self." Jesus "needed to be at-one-d with God, redeemed from sin, raised from death, completed and perfected in holiness, righteousness, and life, just as we, and in the same way and by the same means." He fully shared our humanity and knew "there was no salvation from or out of all death but in and by God." Jesus recognized that "there was only one human way" of salvation; this was "the way of faith," which he perfected.[36]

DuBose urges that Jesus was "not merely to be naturally dominant over an unfallen flesh, but victorious over and resurgent from a fallen flesh."[37] Jesus shared our fallen human nature, and our mortality, including our susceptibility to temptation and the mortal inevitability of death. DuBose states that "the true glory of the Son of Man, as divine representative of men" is "not so much that which entered into Him as endowment as that which is accomplished by Him as human acquirement and attainment."[38] Jesus fully assumed all the propensities and natural consequences of human nature as we receive it. His victory over sin and death is therefore all the more wonderful because his obedience was freely offered in our humanity *"as it is."*[39]

On the other hand, DuBose upholds a real discontinuity between Jesus and the rest of humanity. He emphasizes this theme in many ways in *The Gospel in the Gospels.* Although Jesus' "entire experience in the flesh was a human one, there was yet that in it which transcends all other human experience upon earth."[40] The saving work of the Incarnation "was no mere act of humanity, however exceptional. It was a work wrought by God in humanity. If, on the one side, it was humanity fulfilling or completing itself in God, it was only so because, on the other side, it was equally and primarily God fulfilling and completing humanity in Himself."[41] Without in any way compromising the fullness of Jesus' humanity, DuBose points out the fullness and uniqueness of divinity in the Incarnation. "It does not make our Lord less man to make Him very far more God than any one of us can be, or could become by any degree of human intimacy with the Father."[42]

Jesus' perfected sonship was humanly accomplished, but as an accomplishment it was off the scale of human possibility. Jesus "absolutely transcended the limit of actual or possible human achievement or attainment in the earthly life." Jesus, unlike us, transcends the human experience of "still inhering difference or sin," and "attains here on earth a perfect oneness with the Father, the limit and goal of accomplished sonship." For us, DuBose speculates, this accomplished sonship is only to be perfected "through the grave and gate of death into the fulness of the completed life," involving "we know not what necessary and universal process of natural transformation."[43]

The Universality of the Incarnation in Humanity

Jesus' accomplishment is also exceptional in its significance. DuBose urges that Jesus' humanity was not merely the humanity of an individual man, but rather "the common and universal nature of us all."[44] Therefore Jesus' human holiness, righteousness, and life possess a "universal" significance. Accordingly, Jesus "can be nothing less than God our holiness, our righteousness, our life."[45] Jesus was no mere sample or example of human salvation: "it was not one man but humanity that He was."[46]

The universality of Jesus' human nature is significant for our salvation. Jesus "included all selves in Himself, and suffers, and is crucified and put to shame, or lives anew, rejoices, and is glorified in the whole body and in every member of the humanity that is Himself and His own."[47] Jesus "is present in us every one; and operative unto salvation in every one of us who believes and realizes His presence." The universality of the Incarnation is a distinctive feature of DuBose's christology. In the Incarnation, humanity is saved through Jesus who "is the human, but the divine-human, conqueror and destroyer of sin and of death." Jesus "brought with Him something into our nature and life which was not there before, and raised them into something which was not themselves or their own, and to which they could attain only in and through Him."[48] Jesus' divine-human accomplishment is exceptional, unique, and beyond unaided human possibility.

Condescension and Kenosis in the Incarnation

The christological understanding of "kenosis" is based upon biblical passages such as Philippians 2:6–11, which includes the statement that Jesus

Christ "emptied himself, taking the form of a slave, being born in human likeness." However, Arthur Michael Ramsey points out that the "real source" of the kenotic doctrine of Christ's self-emptying is not the Philippians passage but "consideration of the historical data of our Lord's life considered side by side with the belief in His deity." Kenotic doctrine poses a problem for reconciling Christ's divine and human natures. Despite the assertion of "the dogma of perfect Godhead and perfect Manhood co-existing in the one Person," Ramsey observes that it was "more difficult" "to teach about the incarnate life without making the humanity seem unreal or the deity seem to be ousted by the human limitations."[49]

Kenotic doctrine in christology was a subject of considerable controversy in Anglican theology of the late nineteenth and early twentieth centuries. In 1903 a group of Anglican leaders "explicitly repudiated" any limitation of Jesus' human knowledge by declaring that "since the human mind of our Lord was inseparably united to the eternal word, and was perfectly illuminated by the Holy Spirit in the discharge of his office as teacher, he could not be deceived, nor be the source of deception, nor intend to teach, even incidentally, for fact what was not fact."[50] In contrast, Ramsey notes that Charles Gore, also an Anglican theologian of the time, "reacted with horror from the idea that 'the knowledge infused into the human soul of Jesus was ordinarily and practically equivalent to omniscience.'"[51]

DuBose does not compromise in upholding the fully real humanity of Jesus who shared our human limitations with us. For DuBose, it is precisely in and through the limitations of the human condition that Jesus lived out and completed the way of righteousness that is our salvation. The Scriptures "do not hesitate" to affirm that Jesus "took sin" in the sense that he fully assumed our fallen human nature.[52] DuBose never attributes personal sin to Jesus, but states that Jesus "took sin" only in his assumption of a full humanity with all its propensity and liability to sin. He clearly upholds Jesus' sinlessness, noting that "God was so in Him, the grace of God was so perfected through His faith, that sin was excluded."[53]

DuBose explains that humanity can in mortal life share certain characteristics of God's life, while other aspects of God's life cannot be shared. He urges that "the same love that is the nature of God is the nature of man; the divine reason, will and character may become ours also and must become ours if we are truly to become ourselves." However, DuBose contends, "there is an infinite physical or natural difference between God and us that can never be transcended." He does not ignore the fact that "in the nature of things the Logos cannot cease to be nor can humanity become omnipresent, omnipotent or omniscient." Accordingly, the Incarnation did not violate the natural limits of humanity and the human Jesus was not "omnipresent, omnipotent or omniscient." Therefore, he concludes, it is "absurd" to "speak of the omniscience or omnipotence of our incarnate Lord as though they were a part of the incarnation."[54]

DuBose criticizes "our unworthy fears of compromising our Lord's true divinity and our unworthy desire like Peter to save Him from the extent and consequences of His own utter and (as we think) self-compromising love."[55] Jesus was not tarnished or compromised by accepting the humanity we share in its fullness, including human weakness and susceptibility to sin. The "incarnation and the cross are God not at his lowest but at his highest."[56] The "humiliation of Jesus was His glorification," and "His deepest passion was His highest action, His bitterest suffering His highest perfection, His death for the world the life of the world."[57] DuBose asks, rhetorically, "where else is love so perfect and God so human as in the manger and upon the cross?"[58] He states that "God, like us, can only be compromised by any limitation of His love, *i.e.* of His self-emptying and self-imparting condescension."[59] On the contrary, the self-emptying of kenosis in the Incarnation reveals God's utmost love of us for our salvation. Jesus' embracing the fullness of our human nature did not compromise his divinity, nor did it compromise the integrity of his fully divine and fully human nature. And it did not compromise the perfect moral righteousness of his human personality, as he persisted in freely choosing to live in faith and obedience.

DuBose holds that God's divine loving nature was revealed in and through the human limitations of the Incarnation. "The divinest thing in God is His love, and the love of God is best measured by the depth to which He Himself descended in order thence to raise and exalt us."[60] He finds that, "nowhere else in all God's universe, in all His infinite and manifold activities, is God so God as in the person and work of Jesus Christ. For in Jesus Christ God is all love, and love of all things is most God."[61] Accordingly, "we are not honoring our Lord by limiting His divine condescension of love and trying to make Him more God by making Him less man."[62] More is less, if an overstatement of the role of Jesus' divinity leads to a diminishment of Jesus' humanity and an out-of-balance christology.

At the heart of the limitation and emptying of the Incarnation, we find God's love for us and desire for our salvation. In the Incarnation, "God has indeed descended to us to raise us up to Himself." He has "entered into our impotency to raise it up to his omnipotency."[63] DuBose's position concerning the Incarnation and kenosis recalls Athanasius' dictum as "spokesman for the Eastern tradition that God the Logos had become man in order that men might become God."[64]

Indeed, the lowest humiliation of the cross was the highest moment of God's sacrificial love and generosity for our salvation. DuBose sees a "disposition to measure exaltation by outward circumstances and condition instead of by inward quality and character" in the "hesitation and reluctance to see all God, and highest God, not only in the humanity but in the deepest human humiliation of Jesus Christ." The cross of Christ is the "consummate act" in which "God is most God." In the cross God *is* "the most complete realization and expression of His own divinest nature of love or goodness."[65] DuBose asks, rhetorically, "where before Christ, or where now otherwise than in Christ and in the cross of the divine suffering together with and for man, where in all the story of the universe was or is love so love, or God so God!"[66] The ultimate emptying and humiliation of the cross was the accomplishment of holiness, and obedience, and sonship. DuBose notes, "He who supremely found Himself and found us all is He who the most supremely lost in order to find."[67] The cross was the ultimate expression and realization of God's love for us and our salvation.

Kenosis and Jesus' Human Experience

The emptying and condescension of the Incarnation is evident in Jesus' human life. He "ate, slept, walked as man and so far as his knowledge was natural knowledge and his acts produced physical effects he knew as man and acted as man."[68] In his humanity Jesus' "consciousness was a human consciousness."[69] Jesus "became man in accordance with all the laws and attributes of a real manhood, through a real human birth, infancy and ignorance, growth in knowledge, will and character, faith and obedience, holiness, righteousness and life." DuBose finds that even Jesus' consciousness of "his own higher and eternal nature and preëxistence came to him humanly through his own spiritual intuitions and revelations to him from the Father."[70] Jesus learned and grew in human knowledge and stature, as we all may learn and grow.[71]

It was necessary for Jesus to "*grow* in knowledge, and *begin and finish* the great lesson of faith, and *learn* obedience." DuBose argues that "the Logos, as Logos, would not need to be taught: He would have spoken of Himself."[72] But the child Jesus *did* need to be taught. There were things he did not know. He did not have all the answers. In short, he was not born with human possession of the fullness of divine knowledge. Furthermore, DuBose urges that Jesus' speaking from the first "with the authority of perfect truth does not contradict the fact that He had humanly learned the truth."[73] He explains, "the Logos became man and *was* man. That as man He should have possessed a non-human knowledge and power would have made Him in those respects not man. The Incarnation is not the Logos playing or acting man, or acting through an outward semblance of manhood, but the Logos as man in all the truth and reality of manhood. . . ."[74] His consistent christological perspective relative to Jesus' knowledge and power is that more is less—a more than human knowledge and power on Jesus' part results in a less than fully human being "acting through an outward semblance of manhood."

The question of Jesus' human knowledge and development has everything to do with the reality of the Incarnation. Any masquerade of divine knowledge in human guise would undercut the saving truth that the fullness of human nature was assumed in the Incarnation and redeemed in Christ's victory. Jesus "would have ceased to be man" if any law of human growth and becoming had been "violated or transcended in Him." Similarly, DuBose urges that if "at any point, or in any way" Jesus' human knowledge or power "ceased to be after that mode which we call human, and became what we call divine, then, and in that respect, His humanity was *changed* into divinity."[75] Again, DuBose's christological perspective is that more is less; any departure from the human mode in Jesus' knowledge or growth would have corrupted the assumption of humanity in the Incarnation. Jesus perceives, experiences, and grows in knowledge *humanly*, like us, as he fully shares our humanity.

Jesus' Human Exercise of Free Choice

As Jesus' growth in knowledge was human, his decision making was also in the human mode. Jesus "was a man with a human will and human freedom, who by the grace of God through his human faith overcame sin and destroyed death. . . ."[76] His choices were free human choices. DuBose states rhetorically that if Jesus were a man, and "if the Incarnation is to be taken in earnest," "then assuredly the knowledge, the free will and personal activity, the faith and religious life of Jesus Christ must have been as human as His flesh and bones were."[77] In Jesus we find "the freest and most personal possible" human activity, choice, which is for him as for us "the most determinative and constitutive of our own very selves."[78] For DuBose, to think of Jesus as lacking human freedom of choice "is to think of Him as lacking the essential and the distinction of humanity; it is to rob His human life of all its meaning and truth."[79]

The reality of Jesus' free will concerns the meaning of Jesus' obedience and righteousness. Real obedience requires the possibility of disobedience. If it were somehow impossible for Jesus as the Son of God to sin, then he had no free will and his human obedience was a sham. DuBose explains that the possibility of not obeying was "the very first element and condition" of a "*real* human obedience." Jesus' freedom to choose and his awareness of this freedom were "necessary to the conception of obedience." If Jesus could not sin because of his divinity, if he could not really choose to disobey, "then as God He was incapable of being man and rendering a human obedience."[80] DuBose contradicted an understanding of the Incarnation that would compromise the fullness of Jesus' humanity.

With respect to Jesus' agony at Gethsemane, DuBose notes, "When He Himself says, 'Father, not my will, but Thine be done!' I accept the fact that He was conscious in Himself of two wills, of the necessity of choice between them, and of the possibility of obedience to either."[81] Jesus' prayer at Gethsemane reveals his temptation to choose against God's will; Jesus was sinless, but not immune to human temptation. Jesus was tempted as we are, yet he did not sin. Jesus attained oneness with the Father "for us and therefore as we—not as God but as man, not in the exercise of omniscience and omnipotence, but in the experience of all human weakness and temptation and through the sole power and victory that come from God through faith."[82]

DuBose emphasizes that Jesus' sinlessness was "*His own*," and not the result of a "human nature" that was somehow incapable of sin or impervious to temptation.[83] Whatever such a nature would have been, it would *not* have been human. "Our Lord was not sinless because—in His (in itself) sinless humanity—He was above the touch or reach or power of sin."[84] Jesus' obedience was not inevitable, automatic, or easy—as evidenced by his inner struggle at Gethsemane. Jesus' human nature "was sinless in Him because He was sinless in it, and not *vice versa*."[85] Jesus' human nature "was not the cause of His holiness, but He was the cause of its holiness."[86]

Jesus made human nature holy in the same way that is available to us—by God's grace, through faith. Jesus knew he was not humanly "above the touch or reach or power of sin," and "felt to the very bottom His need of and dependence upon the infinite and eternal Not Himself Who, as the only source of holiness, is the only victory over sin." Jesus recognized his human insufficiency; "there is nothing of Himself that our Lord so emphasizes as His own utter impotence, 'of Himself.'"[87] Because Jesus fully shared the helplessness, impotence, and insufficiency of humanity in the Incarnation, he shows us the way to righteousness. For example, in Jesus' "hours and agonies of doubt and fear" he is "all weakness and dependence: He is all in God just because He is nothing in Himself."[88] Jesus chose to turn from self to faith in God, as we all must in the saving process.

The holiness of Jesus' human nature was through his free obedience and righteousness, which were "identical in kind with *all* human obedience or righteousness."[89] Jesus' victory was a human victory. DuBose explains, "It was the woman's seed, after all, that bruised the serpent's head. It was humanity in Christ that condemned and abolished sin."[90] This victory was won humanly, through Jesus' painful overcoming of sin and human limitation. DuBose urges in *The Gospel in the Gospels* that human holiness must be "wrought out through the pangs and travail of our own free choice and self-determination," and that we cannot "begin to discuss the human holiness of Jesus at all, if we are not to ascribe to Him the formal freedom which is the condition and the essence of our own humanity."[91] This also reflects the kenosis of the Incarnation, because, "as God," Jesus did not "annihilate" the possibility of sin in human nature. Instead, he overcame sin by the exercise of free obedience, "as man."[92] DuBose likewise states that "the divinity of Jesus Christ is seen in the realization and reality of the humanity in which it is incarnate, and not in the displacement of it or the substitution of something else for it."[93]

The Paradox of Jesus' Freedom and the Possibility of Sin

DuBose does nuance his presentation of the possibility of sin by Jesus. He acknowledges the impossibility of sin by the Eternal Logos, for whom "the possibility of sin is a metaphysical absurdity as well as moral blasphemy." Accordingly, if the Incarnation is "construed from the divine side, I confess I see no place for any human formal freedom *(possibilitas peccandi)* in our Lord." He adds that the Divine Logos "could neither have personally erred nor have miscarried or failed in carrying out the divine work of human redemption and salvation."[94] DuBose thus acknowledges the paradox of the Incarnation, admitting that sin by the Divine Logos is unthinkable. Nevertheless, when the Incarnation is construed from the human side, Jesus' formal freedom must be upheld. "DuBose believes that as Christians we are bound to hold to both sides of the dilemma."[95]

Jesus assumed full humanity, including full freedom to choose between obedience and disobedience. Jesus "is the Logos *Incarnate*, become *man* for the very purpose of realizing and revealing the true idea of manhood; *i.e.* of realizing in humanity its true spiritual, moral, and natural actu-

ality or fulfilment of its law, from which the notion of *freedom* is *inseparable.*"
Seen from the human side, Jesus shows how human freedom may "incarnate God" through faith and obedience. This "human side" of the Incarnation was as vital and important as the "divine side," because "we must affirm
the humanity as unequivocally as we do the deity." Incarnation without
human freedom would have been gravely compromised. Accordingly,
DuBose carefully and precisely states that Jesus "is unlike us in the *fact* alone
of His sinlessness, not so in the *mode* of it."[96] The mode of Jesus' sinlessness
was *human.* It involved his freedom, his enduring the real temptations he
experienced, and his own human obedience.

DuBose offers a "both/and" approach to the possibility of sin relative
to the Incarnation. The eternal Logos could not sin, but Jesus, the Logos
incarnated, had real human freedom and could have sinned. His righteousness was *his own.* DuBose's approach may leave something to be desired in
terms of precision and elegance. He offers no simple answer to a very deli-
cate and complex question. But he does provide a balanced, if paradoxical,
answer that upholds both the full divinity and the full humanity of Jesus in
the Incarnation.

Jesus' Lived Experience of Human Righteousness

Jesus' lived experience of human righteousness is at the heart of DuBose's
christology. In *The Ecumenical Councils,* DuBose states that Pope Leo I (d.
461), author of the *Tome to Flavian,* "unconsciously does not hold the completeness of both natures" in Christ. DuBose bases his judgment on the fact
that "there is no really human significance given by Leo to any activity or
experience of our Lord higher than those which are corporeal." In effect, Leo
fails to acknowledge Jesus' human righteousness. DuBose contends that Leo
sees "the reality of our Lord's humanity" in functions "which are not distinctively human at all but only animal," such as "the facts of his hunger, thirst and
weariness." Jesus ate, drank, and slept. These functions "do not even belong
to us distinctively as men."[97]

In contrast to Leo, DuBose holds that Jesus did not merely assume a
human nature "in which it may be possible for deity to undergo experiences
and sufferings of which it is incapable in its own nature."[98] On the contrary,
Jesus not only had the corporeality of a human nature but he also lived a
human righteousness. Jesus' "highest act of faith in God, his supremest
attainment of self-sacrificing love and obedience, his entire conquest of sin
and victory over death, were as truly human acts and activities—and needed
a thousandfold more for our salvation to be truly human—as his merely

bodily passion."[99] This emphasis on Jesus' lived experience of righteousness is consistent with DuBose's attention to the importance of experience in the life of faith. Jesus freely chose the obedience and righteousness that we may choose, by the grace of God. Jesus lived the salvation that we may live, as we live in him and he lives in us. The reality of this process of saving experience would be compromised if Jesus' humanity or his human choices were somehow unreal. DuBose refuses to compromise: Jesus' temptations and struggles were real; his agony at Gethsemane was real; his obedience and righteousness were real. In Jesus, through his freedom, God shared our humanity for love of us and our salvation.

CHRIST THE REVELATION OF SALVATION

We cannot know God "otherwise than as He reveals and imparts Himself," and God "reveals Himself through His own Word and imparts Himself in His own Son."[100] In Christ we see and know "all of God that is communicable to us, or receivable by us."[101] Jesus is the definitive and comprehensive revelation of God, for "all that God has revealed or shall reveal of Himself is expressed in Him."[102] Because he lived the process of salvation completely, Jesus reveals "the energy and the process of our own salvation: God's Word speaking life to us, and God's Spirit answering life in us."[103] Jesus is "the expression to us of what we have to accomplish and become, and of the divine power and way of our accomplishing and becoming it."[104]

DuBose notes that "what is of most consequence in what is revealed" "is not how God may be human but how man may become divine." In this regard, "the former is God's part which we may safely leave to him, the latter is ours and it behooves us to know and perform it."[105] DuBose explains this same point further in the essay "The Subjective and Objective in Religion." He states that we are not so immediately concerned that Jesus "was the pre-eternal divine meaning or intention of us, or that He will be the post-eternal fulfilment and perfection of us," as with "*how*, here and now, in the actual and vital process of being or becoming ourselves, we shall avail ourselves of, appropriate, and make Him ourselves, and make ourselves *Him*."[106] The Incarnation is for our salvation, and our primary concern is *how* we may share salvation in Christ.

As "the sole adequate expression of the divine reason, meaning, and end of human personality," Jesus reveals who and what we are called to be for salvation.[107] He also reveals *how* we are to fulfill this calling. That is, "Jesus Christ is equally the revelation to us of how and what God is in man, and of how and what man is in God."[108] DuBose urges that "Jesus Christ was the Way of Life in both directions, from God to manward and from man to Godward: from God to us He was Love, Grace, Fellowship; from us to God He was Faith, Hope, Love, eternal Life."[109]

Jesus "was God's revelation to us of what and how spiritual and moral manhood are and come to be."[110] It is only in Jesus that "God not merely manifests what He is, but in His activity and self-expression through creation *becomes* what He is." DuBose states that "what God is" and "all that God is" is "not an abstraction of thought, nor is it expressible merely in words." Instead, the divine reality can be known "only in acts."[111] Through Jesus' human experience we may know "what God is."

DuBose holds in *The Gospel in the Gospels* that "God in Himself is love," and that in Christ "the fact of the divine love is consummated and manifested."[112] Again emphasizing the importance of experience, he states, "Love is no more in God than in us an abstract disposition or affection. All the love we know is in concrete relations and the forms of affection determined by the character of those relations."[113] The relationship that Jesus reveals is the "truth of the divine fatherhood realized upon earth by the attainment or accomplishment of human sonship." This love manifests "God's essential disposition" and saving purpose for humanity.[114]

God's love for us is relational. "God is the perfect Self that He can be to us only in that perfection of spiritual relation in which He can be to us the perfection of goodness or love."[115] Jesus is "in Himself the realization and revelation of the divine sonship which is the meaning and proper destination of us all."[116] Jesus "knew the Father through His own perfect realizing of the sonship to God potential in humanity and made actual in Himself."[117] We are to share in this saving relationship of love as we participate in Jesus' perfected sonship. This is the end of the saving process and how it may be fulfilled in human experience. In this regard, DuBose is consistent with his emphases on teleology and the role of human experience in salvation.

Jesus' life reveals the way of salvation in a way that is much more than helpful information or abstract guidance for living. DuBose states, "Christ is more than a revelation to us, of God and ourselves, or our perfect relation. He is not only the truth; but the power, of God and ourselves, and the relation between."[118] Jesus' life in us empowers the completion of the saving process that we see already completed in him. Through his revelation we may subjectively receive and participate in his life, which is to be as effective and victorious in us as it was in him. This is because, "as He was first in His own body so in the bodies of those who are in Him He is the conqueror and destroyer of physical death."[119] Jesus reveals and *is* our salvation.

DuBose notes that "we see in Jesus Christ humanity raised up out of inevitable death in itself into assured and eternal life in God."[120] Jesus thus reveals our "spiritual, moral, and natural end or destination." With respect to teleology, Jesus reveals our human end and meaning in completed at-one-ment with God. "In faith we *have* attained it in Him," DuBose urges, "and through faith we *shall* attain it in Him."[121] Jesus is the effective means for the completion of our salvation.

CHRIST'S WAY OF SALVATION

The Way of the Cross

"The cross" was not just a tragic incident at the end of Jesus' life; it was the "essential thing" in his "human career," and "no mere incident or accident."[122] Nor was the cross merely the wooden instrument of Jesus' death. It was "the only perfect symbol and instrument" of his human life which was "one long and perfect *sacrifice* of the flesh to the spirit."[123] It was the continuous fact of Jesus' loving gift of himself throughout his life. The cross "went with Him from the cradle to the grave, and through every minute of every day." It was "not the fact of a moment but the act of a lifetime." DuBose states that the beatitudes are the revelation of Jesus' "own humanly discovered and humanly experienced secret of blessedness." Jesus' lifelong way of the cross was his drinking "to the bottom" from "the ingredients in the cup" of blessedness.[124] Jesus "had known the poverty which is the condition of the kingdom of heaven, the sorrow without which one cannot experience the divine consolations, the meekness through which He was destined to inherit the earth. . . ."[125] Jesus lived the way of the cross through his whole life; therefore, when he commended it to his followers, he spoke from experience.

The way of the cross is much more than a symbol—it is the way of *our* salvation. DuBose urges that "there is but one way either to Godhead or to the truest manhood—the VIA CRUCIS; and none can come either to the Father or to real selfhood and personality but by it." The cross, "the eternal symbol of self-sacrificing love," is the way "in which God lost and found himself in us and in which we lose and find ourselves in God."[126] The cross of Christ is "*a thing inseparable from human redemption*," and "it means that by which we die to sin and live to God."[127] DuBose explains that "when our Lord enjoins upon *us* the daily use of His cross," he refers to the crucifixion of sin for holiness, righteousness, and life—not the instrument of his death.[128] We may understand from the "person and experience of Jesus Christ" that "the learning, the acquiring and attaining, the accomplishing and becoming" of our own filiation to God "are all impossible without the necessary concomitant of toil, pain, and suffering on our part."[129] The cross is to be our way of salvation.

DuBose emphasizes that the cross is not about suffering for its own sake—sacrifice for its own sake "is still egoistic." In contrast, "genuine self-denial" is forgetful of self. Accordingly, Jesus Christ was and is "the only pure representative of the principle of the cross, or self-sacrifice." It is love, not self-denial or self-sacrifice, that is the "essential principle" of Christ and Christianity, except when love and self-sacrifice are identical.[130] "When our Lord said 'He that hath seen me hath seen the Father' he did not mean that we had seen in him the divine omnipotence or omniscience. We saw something better and higher than that, even the divine love that is not any property of God but God himself, and that we saw raised to its highest power in the incarnation and the cross."[131] It is clear, then, that sufferings "are not in themselves" means of exaltation. Instead, sufferings become the means of our exaltation only "when they are used by God and received by ourselves in the direct line of their final cause or purpose." DuBose explains that "to Christ, and to the spiritual man, all the experiences of life, so far as they are trials at all, are simply parts of the one question of sin or holiness, which is the question of life or death."[132] Our "trials" can thus be moments of self-definition in terms of who we are becoming relative to the process of salvation.

For Jesus, death on the cross was also the completion and perfect final expression of his way of life. His death "was not merely a death, but such a death as fully tested and tried and proved every quality of His life." It "confirmed and perfected" Jesus' "lifelong devotion to the will and work of God." Accordingly, all the New Testament gospels concentrate upon Jesus' death on the cross "as containing and conveying the meaning of all that our Lord was or accomplished upon earth."[133]

In this regard, DuBose upholds a "blood theology" that sees the definitive victory in Jesus' sacrifice on the cross. Our hope for life in Christ is based on sharing the saving benefits of his sacrifice. He explains, "When our Lord's faith and obedience approached its final and completive act upon the Cross, He spoke of it as the 'crisis' of this world— the end of sin and death and hell in humanity as represented in His person—in humanity at large so far as it should be ultimately included in His person. Then was the beginning of the new creation, the restitution: the conquest of sin, casting out of

Satan, and abolition of death."[134] Jesus thus reveals to us that "faith and obedience complete, realize, and fulfil, become *all* themselves only in and through the essential culmination of sacrifice."[135]

The cross is thus the saving instrument by which all that separates us from God may be crucified in us, and we may come to complete the saving process and be at-one with God. DuBose notes that "the essence of the atonement" is "in the fact that humanity taken into God itself dies to and from the sin that separates it from him and lives in the holiness in which it is one with him." The atonement was not performed "externally"; it was "performed for humanity internally." It "was accomplished when humanity in Jesus Christ was made one with God by the spiritual and moral act of the cross," so that "the redemption was finished when in him men overcame sin and destroyed death."[136]

Union with God can come through the cross of pain and suffering. As Jesus' sonship was perfected through sufferings, as he became what he is through sufferings, so our sufferings may be instrumental in the process of our salvation. The most difficult conditions can be the best conditions for the exercise of virtue. The worst environment "demands and elicits the best reaction in order to overcome it." Human conditions "rightly interpreted and rightly acted upon" provide the "best conditions for the production of a divine human life and blessedness."[137] Therefore we should "rejoice in our tribulations," which may teach us the way of the cross and lead to "a more passive patience" and "a more active endurance."[138]

The Experience of Suffering and Evil in the Saving Process

God does not exempt us from suffering, especially from suffering in the process of salvation. God did not "spare" his Son, who "was perfected only through not being spared."[139] And the "divine love will spare man nothing of the need, the effort, the pain, the trial, which are the awful cost of becoming his own highest and divinest self."[140] DuBose explains that "it is the cross that raiseth us; the pain of the world is the lever by which God lifts us to himself."[141] Instead of preventing our suffering as we live and continue in the process of salvation, God loves us and "shares and endures with us and in us, all the extremest conditions and experiences of human life and destiny."[142]

The evil in the world thus may serve a purpose. It provides the occasion for "the holiness, the righteousness, the spiritual and moral life, which are our only natural or supernatural completion, perfection, and blessedness" to come into being "through conflict with and conquest of just that particular evil of the world.[143] DuBose adds that "to the Christian reason, conscience, experience, which sees the profoundest exhibition of the love of the divine Father in the very cross and agony of the infinitely and divinely beloved Son, there is no longer a mystery of evil."[144] The cross is perhaps the greatest of mysteries and contradictions. It is only through the depths and power of Jesus' self-sacrificing love that a hideous instrument of death becomes the means of salvation. We may take up our own cross as we accept the sufferings that come with the saving process.

Concepts of Jesus Expressed through His Titles

DuBose draws on the Letter to the Hebrews, especially Hebrews 2:10 and 12:2, to note various titles and terms for Jesus that give different expressions to his role and activity in our salvation. These christological terms or titles uphold Jesus' humanity. DuBose's use of these terms is consistent with his emphasis on the full humanity of Jesus, and his focus on making the truths of salvation understandable and accessible in terms of human experience.

DuBose notes that Jesus is the "perfecter in Himself, as He will be in us, of that principle in humanity and in human life through which God makes Himself one with us and us one with Him." Jesus is also "the great captain, example and author of our righteousness" who was perfected by those "human experiences, temptations, and sufferings, which are the conditions and natural instruments of all human perfection." Finally, he draws on Hebrews 12:2 (KJV) to note that Jesus is the "'author and finisher,' the leader and consummator, of *faith.*"[145] The faith that saves us "is the human faith perfected and brought to its victory over the world by our Lord Himself."[146]

DuBose also describes Jesus as "an Author and Finisher of the faith of sonship."[147] Jesus was "the forerunner and firstborn, the beginner and finisher, the whole process and *res ipsa*, matter itself," of our glory and salvation. Indeed, DuBose understands the Letter to the Hebrews to be "a description of how Jesus Christ is author and finisher, cause, process, and conclusion of human redemption and completion." Jesus is "the heavenly sanctuary, the dwelling-place of the divine presence in the midst of the sinful people," and "the meeting-place, where God takes the sinner into Himself in His grace, and the sinner takes God into himself through his faith."[148] Jesus is the one who completes the process of salvation.

It is interesting to note that DuBose used the King James translation of the Bible, which renders the Greek *archēgos* in Hebrews 12:2 as "author." Subsequent translations draw out DuBose's meaning even more fully. The Revised Standard Version and the New Revised Standard Version of the Bible both render *archēgos* as "pioneer," describing Jesus as "the pioneer and perfecter of our faith." Jesus was the pioneer because he was the first to complete the way of salvation, which we may share in him. He leads the way, shows the way, and enables us to follow.

In this regard, the Incarnation was not complete at Jesus' birth. It was not "instantaneous"; it was "progressive." The Incarnation was "a process which was complete only in the resurrection and in the spiritual manhood of our Lord as the second Adam. It was not the fact that He was born into humanity merely, but the further fact that in Him humanity was born into God, that made Him, and made man in Him, Son of God."[149] Jesus, our pioneer, is the first to complete the saving process by which our common humanity is "born into God." He is the "perfecter" of our faith. As we follow our pioneer, and live his way, we will be saved.

DuBose draws on Hebrews to describe Jesus as "our high priest who mediates between God and us to the end of effecting our union with God."[150] The annual entrance of the Jewish high priest through the "veil of separation" prefigured and "pointed forward to the act that should forever rend it asunder from top to bottom."[151] Jesus passes through the veil that separates God and humanity, as the Hebrew high priest passed through the veil into the holy of holies of the Jerusalem Temple on the Day of Atonement. Jesus "has opened for us into the holiest place, which is God Himself, a new and living way, through the veil, that is to say, His flesh, and by His blood."[152] Jesus with our shared humanity entered the holy of holies of at-one-ment with God by completing the saving process.

Jesus entered the holy of holies once for all time; in contrast, the Levitical high priest entered the holy of holies once a year, every year, to perform the ritual sin offering. The high priest's annual entrance to the holy of holies only "accentuates" the fact that the separation between God and the people was left unremoved, and symbolizes the necessity for blood to remove the separation. DuBose notes that the high priest "could enter only with *blood*."[153] He explains, "when our Lord died upon the cross, the Veil of the Temple was rent from top to bottom, and the Holy Place was thrown open, which up to that time had been closed, and had barred all entrance to the Mercy Seat, which was the symbol of God's presence; so, by the death of our Lord upon the cross, *the flesh*, our old Adam . . . *all* the barrier which our nature or natural condition interposed between us and God, is rent in twain and swept away, and an open way and free access made for us into God."[154] Jesus fulfilled the meaning of the high priest's annual sacrifice by the one sacrifice of his own blood which removes the barrier between God and humanity. Jesus' one effective sacrifice for sins "for ever" "is the rending of the veil of separation between God and us."[155]

DuBose urges a "blood theology." Jesus resisted "unto blood striving against sin." He "abolished sin in the flesh" by "resisting it unto blood, or unto death, and by the victory over it of His own human holiness in the spirit and power of God through faith." He "needed to be obedient unto the bitter limit of death, and that the most painful and shameful death of the cross." Jesus "entered into the holiest" through "his own blood," and "through the perfect loss or offering up of Himself He eternally found or attained His true Self."[156] DuBose notes that the "unanimity" of the New Testament writers concerning the "supreme significance and necessity of the death of Jesus Christ" leads us to conclude that "the blood of Jesus Christ is the only possible seed of the Gospel or the church."[157]

By his sacrifice Jesus fulfilled and transcended the animal sacrifice that took place at the time of the Levitical high priest's entrance into the holy of holies. Jesus, our high priest, perfected and completed the saving process. Jesus also represents humanity in its relations to God "as man in whom God has fulfilled Himself and who consequently has fulfilled himself in God, through and in a perfect faith, obedience, and life." Therefore, as "the High Priest of humanity," Jesus "embodies the true and perfect concept or notion or truth of humanity."[158]

In Jesus, our high priest, we come to be at-one with God and know God's loving presence. DuBose notes that Jesus has actually brought humanity "into a real oneness with God." Our at-one-ment with Jesus includes the "divine-human *sympathy*" of our relationship with him. By the "perfect sympathy" of the relationship we share with him, he is "infinitely nearer" than he would be if he "were still present in the flesh." As our high priest, "we recognize in Him the revelation to us of ourselves, but of ourselves not as we are, but as we shall be when we have truly become ourselves."[159]

Jesus lived the way of salvation and makes it possible for us to share it as we live in his experience and he lives in ours. The loving sacrifice of salvation is the way of the cross, which was completed and opened for us in Jesus' life. Christ is the reality, the way, and the ongoing process of human salvation. Thus, the saving Incarnation includes us as Christ's life is fulfilled in us and our life is fulfilled in him.

Christ as the One Who Embodies Completed Salvation

Jesus empowers our union with God as well as embodying it. Faith "makes Jesus Christ very much more than a mere example to us: it makes Him not only sample but cause and substance of our salvation."[160] Jesus "gives Himself to us, not only as sample or example, as evidence and proof of what God would do with us and in us—if we will—but as the effectual power and substance of it."[161] Jesus' life, the objective offer and power of our salvation, is what we are to live, and in him we have the power to do so. Therefore Jesus "is in Himself that which we are to become—which already in grace and in anticipating faith, though not yet in accomplished fact, we *have* become— in Him."[162] Knowing Christ is "our Gospel," and "the being what He is our salvation," because "everything essential to our being ourselves, performing our parts, and achieving our ends, we see realized and illustrated in the person of Jesus Christ."[163]

Jesus embodies the completion of the process that saves us. He is also "the realized ideal of human nature, human life, and human destiny."[164] Jesus is the living human fulfilment of our saving relationship with God. In Jesus, filiation is perfected by grace through perfect faith and obedience. DuBose understands our destiny in terms of evolutionary process and the teleology of Aristotle. He states, "I believe Jesus Christ to be the revelation of the true meaning, and the realization of the true destination of every man; and that in Him as the personal incarnation and reproduction of the personal God in our personal selves we and the whole creation shall come into our divine inheritance."[165] Our destiny is our destination, which we see in Jesus who completes and fulfills the evolutionary process.

JESUS CHRIST THE WAY OF OUR SALVATION

The focus of saving christology must be on the human way of salvation that Jesus lived, revealed, and empowers. DuBose urges that "the Gospel of Jesus Christ is the Gospel of the Way—the way to God, the way into the Holy of Holies, the way of holiness and righteousness and eternal life." The acknowledged "divine Sonship which incarnated itself in Jesus Christ" still "had to realize or actualize itself by the necessary course and process of human sonship." *How* Jesus humanly acquired this sonship is the usual focus of the New Testament, even though the New Testament likewise assumes Christ's "eternal personal pre-existence," his "eternal sonship in Himself to the Father," and his identity as "eternal Logos" and "eternal Son of God." Accordingly, with respect to Jesus, "the main point for us is rather the *how* than the *what* of His sinlessness." Similarly, how Jesus "*became* Son as man," rather than "how our Lord *was* Son as God" is the subject of the Letter to the Hebrews.[166]

Jesus' way was the human way of faith and obedience, "the way in which alone human holiness is possible, by union through faith of God with Himself and of Himself with God." Jesus thereby "opened and established a way of holiness not for Himself alone but for all in Him."[167] His life was a human victory of *faith*. DuBose emphasizes that "Jesus Christ was sinless *through faith*, and rose from the dead *through faith*, and was one with God, and obeyed His law, and lived His life *through faith*."[168] We likewise are to share that saving faith. It is only "the absence or incompleteness of our faith" that "stands between us and everything else" needed for our salvation.[169]

Jesus' life and victory was for all humanity. DuBose explains that throughout Jesus' life "He was accomplishing something greater than raising His body from the grave. From beginning to end He was the spiritual and moral resurrector and resurrection of the human nature in which He lived."[170] The "resurrection of His body from the dead was but the outward consequence of His having raised humanity in His own person out of spiritual and moral death."[171] His death and resurrection "reveal Him to us" as "the end of all religion from the beginning, and the predestination of humanity in God."[172] DuBose certainly believes in the bodily resurrection of Christ, but he likewise holds that "the physical resurrection is merely the outer and visible side of a great spiritual and moral act on our Lord's part." Jesus' victory was humanity's victory over sin and death. "If He, being what we are, has come to God, then we know by Him our way to God."[173] Jesus "drank the cup and was baptized with the baptism which we must drink and be baptized withal, if we would be where and what He is."[174]

Jesus' victory is our victory as we receive it and participate in it. As humanity's way to God, Jesus is "second Adam," who reverses the fall that took place in Adam and restores "our lost liberty and life." As Adam reveals the way of each person's fall, so Christ, the second Adam, reveals the way of humanity's return to God. The great significance of Jesus' resurrection is not just in the raising of *his* body from the dead, but in the raising of *humanity* to salvation. We share personally in this "coming or bringing back of all men in Him" as we are "partakers of His holiness and life."[175]

The Role of Miracles in Christ's Mission: An Ambivalent Perspective

DuBose was "no advocate of miracles."[176] He states, "no one can say that the bringing of dead men back to physical or natural life again, or even of sick men to physical health again by other than natural means, is any part of the essential, permanent, and universal health and life giving work of Christ. Whatever necessary purpose those miracles served was an occasional, temporary, and non-essential one and ought not to be included in the permanent operation of our religion."[177] It is interesting to note that DuBose does not state his disbelief in the Gospel accounts of Jesus' miracles. But he is concerned that the miracles may present a "stumbling-block" to contemporary thought and conscience because of "the world's growing observation and experience of the inviolability and uniformity of natural law."[178] In this regard, DuBose does seem to have capitulated to the rational and skeptical spirit of his time concerning the miracles of Jesus.

DuBose tends to marginalize the importance of Jesus' miracles in his endeavor to show the consistency of Christian faith with the scientific methods and theories of his time. It may be that Jesus' miracles seemed out of place to DuBose in a world that was discovering the truths of empirical and historical-critical research. In this regard, D. S. Cairns wrote in 1928 that "there is no doubt that in our day the Modernist criticism of miracle is mainly due to its apparent conflict with physical science." Cairns adds that the Modernists include "deeply religious men" who "believe that any conflict between science and religion must needs be a supreme disaster."[179] Although it does not appear that DuBose viewed the miracles as "a supreme disaster," his response to them was certainly guarded.

DuBose offers different explanations for the miracles. The miracles were for initial effect, reflecting Jesus' need "to produce an adequate impression upon the hearts and minds of men of not only His disposition and mission but also of His authority and power to be the divine helper and healer." DuBose distinguishes this from Jesus' mission and "permanent function" to "treat causes," "to take away sin, and by consequence all the consequences of sin." It was not Jesus' purpose to treat symptoms, "and symptoms only indirectly, as they could be temporarily alleviated."[180]

DuBose also suggests that the appearance of the miraculous may simply reflect our own less than complete knowledge of the natural. He states, "we assume that if we understood all facts, all facts would appear to us as natural." He finds that with the growing "observation and experience of the inviolability and uniformity of natural law," miracle "has gradually disappeared, not, assuredly, because facts have changed, but because our understanding and interpretation of facts have changed." DuBose notes that he "should very much prefer to believe" that Jesus' miracles manifest "some higher natural working than we have as yet been able to correlate with what we so far know of nature." For example, he suggests, the "extraordinary powers" Jesus possessed to perform "the works we call miracles" may reflect "psychic and spiritual forces as yet latent in human nature of which we know not whereunto the future development may reach."[181] In this respect he offers what is basically a "rational" explanation for Jesus' miracles.

DuBose did not encourage a Christian faith that was founded on the spectacular or fantastic. He finds that the "world still wants miracle in its Christianity, to the untold damage of itself and the utter contradiction of Christianity." He also notes "the misapprehension that the true supernatural is a condemnation or in any respect whatever a supplanting or displacing of the natural." Instead, the "true supernatural is only the truer and higher natural." DuBose is "loath to believe that what I consider the most significant, beneficent, and interpretive event in creation should have been interjected into it as an interference or amendment."[182] Because the strong emphasis of DuBose's christology was on the human righteousness of Jesus, he was deeply suspicious of a piety that yearned for other-worldly solutions as a substitute for personal righteousness. Accordingly, DuBose holds that "the whole work of God is one and of a piece, that addition or interference or reparation from without would be a confession of imperfection or failure," and that the "natural has become to us more divine than the non-natural or the contra-natural." With respect to Jesus' "higher generation" and resurrection, he notes that the "highest acts or events in the earthly history of God or nature or man" are not "miracles in any objectionable sense." Instead, when they shall be viewed "in the light of their sufficient reasons, or causes," they "shall be known to be the most natural of facts, because they are the real acts, events, and ends for which nature itself exists."[183]

On first impression, DuBose's position on Jesus' miracles seems inconsistent with the rest of his christology. He believed in the fullness of Jesus' divinity and humanity in the Incarnation, which certainly represented a break from natural laws as they were understood. Furthermore, he was deeply influenced by his mystical conversion experience as a cadet, and he clearly did not deny the supernatural as such. However, DuBose's understanding of the miracles *is* ultimately consistent with the rest of his theological system of salvation. In terms of *exitus et reditus*, all creation comes from God and all creation is to return to God in the fulfilment of the saving process. Creation, God's plan for salvation, the saving process, the destined and intended end of all creation in God—these are all ultimately "of a piece" for DuBose. God's saving activity in the Incarnation is therefore not an intrusion into the order of nature, but rather an expression of God's love for our salvation that is entirely consistent with the creation, meaning, and intended end of nature. The "whole process of death and resurrection, of regeneration, and of eternal life instituted and inaugurated by Jesus Christ" is "in the higher and the highest sense a natural one." This process "includes not only the beginnings of spiritual life here, but the completion of physical or natural life hereafter."[184] In this regard, we may say that DuBose challenges the usual definition of miracle rather than the reality of miraculous events such as Jesus' resurrection.

DuBose adopts a stance that may be characterized as "reverent agnosticism" concerning *how* the resurrection happened. He emphasizes the "overwhelming spiritual probability with which through all the life of Jesus we have come at last to the necessity of His resurrection." For DuBose, Jesus' resurrection was necessarily tied to his sinlessness and holiness. The "all-important and all-inclusive truth" of the resurrection allows us "to pass by the natural and scientific difficulties as exceptional, and . . . non-essential." We may therefore excuse ourselves from the "side issue" of "reconciling the facts of the spirit with those of matter."[185]

DuBose's ambivalence concerning "miracles" does not signify a lowering of the divine in the Incarnation. For DuBose, Jesus is not just a righteous human being whose saving gift is merely salvation by sample. On the contrary, the life of Christ "is higher than nature can carry us, or than we can carry ourselves in our own fulfilment of the law of nature," and "not therefore contrary to nature." We cannot be completed by nature alone, and we are not "able of ourselves to fulfil the law of self-completion." But we can "find the completion at once of our nature and ourselves in highest union and association with God." Our saving participation in the Incarnation is "our own highest nature," and "the true supernatural."[186] DuBose urges us to redefine our customary understandings of nature and miracle to see the unity of creation, the saving process, and the destined end of all things in at-one-ment with God. Salvation is the intended end and completion of our nature in loving union with God, not a magical interruption or violation of nature by an alien force.

DuBose firmly upholds the fullness of Christ's divinity and humanity, and the unity of Christ's divine and human natures. Although careful to present a balanced christology, he also seeks to counter what he perceives to be a long-standing tendency of Christian theology to diminish Jesus' humanity. Such an out-of-balance christology, tipped to exaggerate the divinity, leads to an out-of-balance soteriology in which the role of human participation in the saving process (for Jesus and for us) is not fully appreciated.

DuBose emphasizes that Jesus humanly completes and embodies the saving process. Jesus' righteousness is a human righteousness. His faith and obedience are human faith and obedience. Jesus lives the way of salvation that we are to live. He was not an otherworldly being in the guise of a man.

His righteousness was lived out in our humanity, which he fully assumed with all our human weaknesses, limitations, and susceptibilities. Realizing his own human limitations, and turning from self to God, Jesus received divine assistance by the Spirit to live a perfect human righteousness.

DuBose fully embraces the "scandal" of the Incarnation—that God the son became man for love of us and our salvation. Jesus experienced human life, temptation, and death. His inner struggle at Gethsemane and his suffering on the cross were not charades. He experienced the saving process to the full, lived a human righteousness, and reveals to us how we may share his human life/death/resurrection experience. DuBose also embraces the paradox of Jesus' human freedom. This is another distinctive aspect of his christology. Although it is unthinkable that the divine Son could have sinned or failed, yet (humanly speaking) Jesus had the same freedom to choose between obedience and disobedience that we all share. Indeed, Jesus' righteousness was a human righteousness only if he (like us) could freely choose to obey or disobey. The reality of Jesus' human righteousness meant the way of the cross for him, which is to be the way we share. Jesus *is* our salvation. His life in us is the objective and saving offer that includes us in the Incarnation. By grace through faith, by living the way of righteousness that Jesus reveals, the objective gift of salvation can be actualized as our subjective reality. Following his way, we may know the accomplished relation of at-one-ment with God.

For DuBose, creation, the saving process, and the destiny of all things for at-one-ment with God are "of a piece" and all part of nature in its highest sense. Seen in this light, the Incarnation and Jesus' resurrection are not intrusions into the natural order but expressions of nature's highest reality and meaning. Throughout his christology, DuBose emphasizes that the way of salvation is the way of righteousness that Jesus actually lived. Our salvation is not to be sought in spectacular intrusions from beyond the natural order. God does not displace our human freedom and capacities in the process of salvation. God does not relegate us to a passive stance. Jesus freely and humanly revealed the life of faith, love, obedience, righteousness, and sacrifice that we are to share for salvation.

CHAPTER 4

The Spirit

For DuBose, the Holy Spirit is often the point of synthesis or junction where the different facets of theology come together in a very dynamic way. DuBose describes the Spirit as (1) active for our salvation in concert with the Word, (2) active in cooperation with Jesus' human obedience and faithfulness in the saving process, (3) active in us as we follow Jesus' way and receive the Spirit in faith, and (4) active as the principle of unity, community, and Jesus' effective presence in the church. His concern with pneumatology reflected the growing interest in theology of the Spirit that was emerging in the nineteenth and early twentieth centuries. He also anticipated the much greater attention that pneumatology would receive from theologians in the latter part of the twentieth century.

THE MISSION OF THE SPIRIT AND THE MISSION OF THE WORD

DuBose is explicitly trinitarian in his emphasis on the cooperation of Word and Spirit in the saving process. He states that "*all* God's operations in us as spiritual beings are by the word through the spirit." Relative to the Son, we see the Spirit's activity "in the preparation of the world for His coming; in His actual coming and manifestation of Himself in our flesh; and in the extension of His incarnation and impartation of Himself to us through the church as His body." Relative to the Father, DuBose notes that "it is not possible to know God except in Trinity . . . without us by His Word, and within us through His Spirit."[1] In this regard, DuBose closely parallels the trinitarian understanding of the English theologian R. C. Moberly (1845–1903), who states, "No one can have the Spirit, and not thereby have the Father and the Son: neither is there any other conceivable possibility of having the Father and the Son, save in, and as, personally indwelling Spirit."[2]

We know God only through Word and Spirit. DuBose holds that the "divine Word or Son who objectively reveals or expresses Him to us, and the divine Spirit who subjectively communicates or imparts Him in us, are the only possible media of any direct knowledge or experience of God." With respect to the prologue of the Gospel of John, he states that the "life of God and of Jesus Christ His Son, is in us by impartation and participation of His Spirit." He likewise explains, "The function of the promised Holy Ghost was to be that He should 'take of the things of Jesus, and show them unto us.'"[3]

DuBose also presents a trinitarian understanding of the objective/subjective process of salvation. God's *subjective* activity for our salvation is appropriated by the Spirit, the third Person of the Trinity, just as God's *objective* activity for our salvation is appropriated by the Word, the second Person of the Trinity. The "Divine *Word* is the principle of objective revelation and communication from God to man," as "the *Holy Ghost* is the principle of subjective reception and appropriation on the part of man from God."[4]

The missions of Word and Spirit are both needed for the revelation of God that saves us. DuBose warns that "if there is no Spirit of God within, there is for us no Word of God without."[5] He likewise states that God is "unknowable and incommunicable but through Christ," but that Christ is only the "self-revelation and self-communication of God" to us "through the coequal action of the Holy Ghost." Similarly, he notes that "it is only God within us that can make us receptive of God without us; no man can come to the Word except he be drawn by the Spirit."[6] Our subjective reception of the objective gift of salvation is made possible by the Spirit.

DuBose is once again close to R. C. Moberly in identifying the necessity of the Spirit's role in our saving knowledge of the Son. In a discussion of Jesus' promise in his farewell discourse that the Father would send "another Comforter" to his disciples (John 14:16–20), Moberly notes that "it is not for an instant that the disciples are to have the presence of the Spirit *instead of* having the Son." On the contrary, "to have the Spirit *is* to have the Son."[7] The Spirit makes the Word present, knowable, and effective for our salvation. The Spirit does not displace or marginalize the Word.

The Holy Spirit empowers our salvation in many ways. DuBose notes that "in the conception and birth of our Lord Himself, in the spiritual birth of baptism, in the spiritual life of the Eucharist, it is always *the Word by the Spirit*."[8] This reflects the ongoing cooperation of the missions of the Son and the Holy Spirit in the saving process. Therefore "as eternal life is given to us in Jesus Christ to be received, so is it given to us by the Holy Ghost to receive the life."[9] By the Spirit we receive salvation in Christ.

With respect to the complementary missions of Word and Spirit for our salvation, DuBose notes that "as in the grace of the Word there is a gift not from ourselves, so in the grace of the Spirit there is a reception not by ourselves." The power of the Gospel for our salvation requires both its "objective communication," and "a corresponding subjective response." The Gospel must therefore be for us "equally and coördinately," one "of Word and of Spirit."[10] The objective gift of salvation in Christ is to be realized by grace through faith. The Holy Spirit is the means for our realization by enabling our subjective appropriation of salvation. DuBose explains, "The whole prevenient and subsequent function of the Holy Ghost is subjective. In itself it reveals nothing and communicates nothing: it only prepares *us* for what shall be or has been revealed and communicated. The revealer and communicator is *the Word*."[11] In *The Ecumenical Councils*, DuBose explains that the objective mission of the Son and the subjective mission of the Holy Spirit work together. "The function of the Word appears in the divine impartation, that of the Spirit in the human susceptibility and reception. By the Word God begets, by the Spirit humanity conceives and bears; through both God is incarnated and humanity is regenerated and redeemed."[12] Both Word and Spirit are essential in the saving process.

We are included and saved in the Incarnation through the Word and the Spirit. DuBose explains that the Spirit prepares and enables humanity "to incarnate, or be the incarnation of, the Divine Word."[13] In *The Gospel in the Gospels*, he notes that Word and Spirit work together for the divine sonship to be born in us "of the Word and the Spirit," with "the Word being the objective divine expression to us of the truth of sonship, and the Spirit the subjective divine realization in us of the fact of sonship."[14]

By the Word, salvation in Christ is *for* us. By the Spirit, salvation in Christ is *in* us, and *ours*. By the Spirit, the salvation that is objectively true and complete in Christ becomes an increasing subjective reality in our lives. By the Spirit, we advance in the saving process so that the "already" of objective life in Christ becomes increasingly our own. DuBose's description of the role of the Spirit in the saving process is a distinctive feature of his theology of the Spirit. It is also consistent with his emphasis on the role of human experience in the saving process and in theological reflection. The Spirit enables and empowers us to receive Christ and live the process of salvation. The Spirit also enables and empowers us to recognize and realize the truths of Christian faith in our lives. The saving process is actualized by the Spirit.

SPIRIT CHRISTOLOGY

DuBose presents a "spirit christology" that emphasizes Jesus' participation in the same process of salvation that is available to all persons. The process of salvation is completed in Jesus, both objectively and subjectively. Christ "is both God *salvum faciens* and man *salvus factus*, both the Logos by the Holy Ghost *saving* and man by the Word through the Spirit *saved*."[15] Jesus' human holiness, righteousness, and life were realized for him—as they can be for us—by grace through faith. By the Spirit, Jesus humanly lived the same process of salvation that saves us. His was "the highest faith," which humanly cooperated with "the most real activity of the eternal Spirit, whose part in us we call grace."[16] But Jesus' way of salvation was not a higher way than ours. Jesus received and cooperated with the Spirit in the saving process, just as we must. "If the Spirit of God operated more powerfully, even perfectly, in Him, it was precisely in the ratio in which, humanly, He cooperated most perfectly with the Holy Ghost."[17]

It is significant that Jesus' holiness was not the inevitable result of a sinless human nature. Jesus' holiness "was of the Holy Ghost *in Him*, and not merely *in His nature*." In this regard, DuBose notes Jesus' "use and need of faith and prayer, and His sole dependence upon the Holy Ghost and divine grace." Jesus' "personal faith and obedience as man" did not result from "the necessary sinlessness of His divine self as Second Person of the Trinity, but the voluntary sinlessness of His human self by the Third Person of the Trinity."[18]

Similarly, Jesus' divine power and knowledge as man were "the communicated divinity of the Third Person of the Trinity, and not the original or underived divinity of the Second Person." By the Spirit, Jesus humanly received divine assistance from beyond himself. And by the Spirit, he freely chose and lived the path of righteousness. Jesus' life reveals our path of salvation by manifesting his full reception of the Holy Spirit and his freely chosen human righteousness. Jesus received the Spirit and participated in the saving process through perfect faith. The Holy Spirit was active and present in Jesus "without measure, because His own faith and obedience were without measure." "Equally," Jesus' faith was "without measure" because "the Holy Ghost was given to Him without measure." The fullness of Jesus' righteousness and the fullness of the gift and presence of the Holy Spirit to him were each "cause" and "effect" of the other.[19] By faith, through the Spirit, we too may be included in the saving process of the Incarnation.

THE SPIRIT, GRACE, AND HUMAN ACTION

DuBose emphasizes that the saving process which Jesus experienced is the way for our salvation. As Jesus receives the Holy Spirit and lives "in the Spirit," the Spirit enables his human holiness. Holiness is the "distinctive quality of Christian character and life," and "all holiness is of the Holy Ghost."[20] By the Spirit, we are able to follow Jesus in holiness. By the Spirit, we follow the Son. Our human fulfilment and salvation are empowered by the activity of the Spirit.

DuBose's "spirit christology" concerns the entire process of the Incarnation. It is not restricted to Jesus' life. Jesus "taught that His own function as the Word was to be not superseded, but succeeded and completed by that of the Spirit." The Spirit "was not to supply His absence but to effect His presence" in a "much more real and effectual" way.[21] It is through the Spirit that we may be included in the Incarnation for our salvation. In the Nicene Creed "the words 'was incarnate' do not mean the isolated initial act only of His physical conception and birth, but the whole process of His so entering into humanity as to be its incarnation of the Divine Logos as well as the Divine Logos so incarnate in it."[22] By the Spirit, we may be included in the entire process of the Incarnation.

The Spirit enables our hearts to receive God's love by subjectively preparing us to accept God's offer of salvation. The Spirit makes salvation-in-Christ objectively present to us, and makes possible the subjective completion of the saving process in our lives. DuBose explains, "Christ can be personally *in us*, as our subjective life, only by the Holy Ghost in us as the principle and power of *our own* personal appropriation and reproduction of Him."[23] As "our subjective qualification to receive the things that be of God," the Spirit gives us "eyes to see, and ears to hear, and hearts to understand, and minds to know."[24] In other words, the Spirit "manifests Himself in *our* power to receive and to live Christ; His is the power by which our Lord enables all who believe in Him to become children of God." Throughout "the whole process of the coming of the Son of God into our nature and into ourselves," the Holy Spirit is "the principle and agent" who prepares and enables humanity for the "spiritual conception and birth in it of the objective Word of God."[25]

It is only through the Spirit that we may "enter into living relation" with the objective truth of God beyond us by making a "response of correspondence." That correspondence is itself "an act of spiritual communication or self-impartation" by the Spirit. DuBose notes, "When the Spirit bears witness with our spirit, that we are sons of God, it is not only God who communicates the gracious fact, but it is God who awakens the humble and grateful response, and puts it into our heart to say, Abba, Father."[26] God's giving and our receiving are both through the gift of the Spirit. The objective and saving reality beyond us must become a subjective reality in "living relation" with us. God can be "*our* God only as He is conceived in us by the operation of the Spirit of God and born of the want which He implants and the faith which He generates."[27]

Participation necessarily involves cooperation. Our cooperation is made possible by grace, which is the active presence of the Spirit in our lives. Grace calls for *free* cooperation. Although grace has "an objective reality" that is "apart" from us, it operates reasonably and naturally in our lives. Grace "appeals to and makes use of and fulfils itself through all the familiar elements and faculties of our nature, intelligence, affection, desire, will, and activities, so that the actions of grace are all equally the actions of ourselves acting rationally and naturally."[28] DuBose describes one of the definitions of grace as "the work in us of the Holy Ghost, through Whom, in sequence and conjunction with the Word, are mediated all those divine operations upon the earth that we might characterize as subjective," serving to "draw, or fit, or assimilate" the subjects of this activity to God, "and make them in their measure partakers of His nature."[29]

Salvation is freely offered in Christ, and is to be freely received by us. No one can be saved against his or her will. DuBose states, "if God be truly in me by His Word and His Spirit, He is so not to supplant or to displace my nature or my personality, but only to complete them on their own lines and perfect them in their own activities."[30] The Spirit does not take away our freedom to deny salvation; we may refuse to participate in the saving process. The Spirit invites and enables us to receive the gift that saves us.

But our salvation is not otherworldly or alien to us. Our union with God does not displace our human personality or gifts. As DuBose notes, "God Himself cannot, by power working necessarily and immediately, work a righteousness in us, for then it would be no more a righteousness than the straightness of a stick or the movement of a falling body is a righteousness." We must cooperate freely in the completion of the saving process, "as *we* can," by grace through faith.[31]

There is "a divine self-impartation or grace which works through our faith and transforms us from what we are into what God is and would become in us.[32] There is thus a mutuality of divine and human activity in the working out of our salvation. DuBose holds that "we are not saved *fide sola*, by faith alone." Nor are we saved by grace alone, because grace can only operate "in and through faith." Grace and faith must work together in cooperation and correspondence. As "potential grace" becomes "actual grace" only through our faith, "so, on the other hand, the subjective reaction of faith is nothing in itself or except in correspondence with the objective reality and power of grace."[33]

DuBose explains that grace is the "mode of the divine operation upon *persons*, as distinguished from *things*; and faith is the condition in *persons* of the divine operation in or upon them." Accordingly, grace is "not, like other power, necessary in its effects, but contingent upon the conscious will and the willing obedience, that is, upon the faith, of its subject or recipient." He urges that "the working of the Spirit is always and only manifested in the subjective disposition and activity, in the free self-surrender, receptivity, and co-working of that in and with which it works."[34] The Holy Spirit does not overwhelm us in the saving process; rather, our salvation is to be actualized and completed by grace through faith. Through grace we may receive what we could never have effected through our own strength and initiative.

With respect to our experience of subjective revelation, DuBose states, "we may for a long time know spiritual facts without us, and then suddenly come to an interior knowledge of them so different from and transcending the other that it seems to be a difference in kind as well as in degree." It is this "difference in kind" that enables us to distinguish objective manifestation from subjective revelation, and to discern the activity of the Spirit. This is the difference between "knowing about" spiritual things and "knowing them," made possible by "the light that is within us." It is "this interior light, the vision of the spiritual man for the spiritual thing, that is the function of the Spirit."[35]

The offer of salvation always precedes our reception of it. In this process, we "lay hold upon grace because grace has laid hold upon us."[36] The action of the Holy Spirit "is cause of, and not merely consequent upon, the human motions of our own spirits."[37] Grace comes first, preveniently making our response in faith possible. DuBose states, "*we* actually begin to become spiritual only from the point when God's Spirit begins to work *with* ours through the working of *ours* with His; but before that *He* is moving though we be not moved."[38] This cooperation means that we are drawn into deeper and deeper relationship with God for our salvation.

We cannot free ourselves by a "natural" act on our own initiative from "the slavery and bondage of the flesh." But we can "*be freed* from it" by "the power and activity of the Holy Ghost in us, through our own faith, obedience, and personal, spiritual, and moral, activity." We cannot save ourselves. But as the grace and power of Christ's death and resurrection become our own through the impartation of the Spirit, we can be saved.[39]

OUR SALVATION IN THE SPIRIT THROUGH THE CHURCH

We are not alone or isolated as we participate in the missions of the Spirit and the Son. DuBose identifies the Spirit with the "*koinonia* of ourselves with God in Christ." The Spirit calls us together as the church. As the Spirit is "the unity in Heaven of Father and Son," the Spirit is likewise on earth "the bond between God and us, that bond revealed, consummated, assured to us in Jesus Christ."[40] Thus, the Spirit is the effective means of our fellowship with God in Christ, and with each other in him. DuBose characterizes the "first half of the New Testament" in terms of Christ's "accomplishing our sonship, effecting our redemption and resurrection from sin and death, entering upon our inheritance of eternal life." But the "second half of the New Testament is the promised ministry of the Holy Ghost—'taking of the things of Jesus and showing them' to His church."[41]

DuBose continually returns to the ecclesial dimension of salvation. He notes that the promise of "a permanent possession of the truth" was given to the church, not to individual believers, and "this promise was to be made good by the presence with the church of the Holy Ghost, through whom, as God was in Christ, so Christ was to be spiritually present with the church to the end of time."[42] Salvation is available to us in the life and sacraments of the church through the Spirit. This is a basic conviction for DuBose, who states, "I believe in a present God in Christ by the Holy Ghost saving, regenerating, and sanctifying the world *through the Church*."[43]

The Spirit acts through the sacraments. For example, DuBose notes that "every true baptism is an integral part of the divine act or process of incarnation." He likewise urges that every baptism is "at least in its divine intention and meaning, as much the personal act of Jesus Christ as the Virgin birth was the act of the Divine Word. In both cases it is by the Holy Ghost."[44] The missions of both Son and Spirit are involved in the sacraments of the church.

If we deny or reject the church's life and sacraments, we can distance ourselves from the saving benefits that are available through the Spirit in the church. DuBose notes that "all the weakness of the church to regenerate, sanctify, and save is the inability of Christ through our want of faith."[45] There is nothing "magical or superstitious" in the presence of "God in Christ by the Holy Ghost" through "the church and its functions."[46] We must participate in the life and sacraments of the church, by grace through faith. The life and ministry of the church is empowered by the Spirit who invites and enables our free participation in the saving process.

True to his emphasis on lived experience, DuBose describes the activity of the Holy Spirit in terms of the subjective clarity of spiritual knowledge evidenced by the disciples after Pentecost, and in terms of the subjective inner clarity that we may know. With respect to the Pentecost event, he notes that the "vague and indefinite emotions" of the disciples were replaced by "a clear understanding and a definite plan and purpose as to the meaning and the preaching of Christ and the resurrection." DuBose urges that this "surprising change" on the Day of Pentecost cannot be treated as "artistic literary fiction."[47] This "surprising change" reflected the subjective preparation and activity of the Spirit. It is by the Holy Spirit that Christ is actively and effectively present in the church's life and sacraments for our salvation. The Holy Spirit is the *means* for the saving process to be active and effective in our lives, and in the life and sacraments of the church.

The Spirit empowers the saving process in Jesus' experience, and in ours. By the Spirit, Jesus lived in obedience and righteousness to fulfill the meaning of divine sonship in his human life. Jesus recognized his human limitation, and received divine assistance by the Spirit for the completing of salvation. In the same way, the Spirit enables *us* to participate in the saving process which leads to at-one-ment with God. The Spirit makes available to us the objective gift of salvation in Christ. It is likewise the Spirit who enables our subjective and personal reception of that gift so that salvation in Christ may become a reality in us.

The Spirit makes Christ present in our lives, and in the life and sacraments of the church. It is the Spirit who draws us together in the one body of Christ, which is the life of the church and our hope. By the Spirit's making-present to us of salvation in Christ, and by our faithful participation in the saving process which the Spirit empowers, we are *saved*.

CHAPTER 5

The Church

Christ is made present for our salvation by the Spirit in the life and sacraments of the church. DuBose's christology and soteriology culminate in his ecclesiology. In this regard, we may note that the last three chapters of *Soteriology* concern his theology of the church. They are titled "Of Salvation in the Church," "Of Baptism," and "Of the Lord's Supper." For DuBose, it is most especially in and through the church that we encounter Christ by the Spirit for our salvation.

THE INCARNATION IN THE CHURCH

DuBose urges a radical identification of Christ and church, because "in the mind and heart and will of God *we* are the body of Christ and the subject of the Incarnation." God is near at hand for DuBose. He warns that "our Christianity is too far off from us; we think of the Incarnation of God and the presence of Christ as too exclusively in heaven, and not sufficiently on earth and in ourselves."[1] Christ "is practically and actually in this world of ours only in and with and through His Body the Church."[2] The "work of Christ is the work of the Church" and "is waiting upon the Church for its accomplishment."[3] DuBose's radical identification of Christ with the church places great responsibility on the members of the church for working God's purposes in the world. "'God in Christ' does nothing whatever in or for the world that is not done in, with, through, and by us who are the members and organs of His bodily presence and operation upon each."[4]

DuBose holds that the church is the means by which the objective and sacramental presence of Christ continues among us and in our lives. He urges that "the Church and the Sacraments have no other significance than the continued presence of Jesus Christ Himself upon earth, and our human part and participation in Him."[5] This radical identification of Christ with the church means that the "Church is as much the sacrament of His Presence, as His human Body was of the Presence, the Incarnation, of God in Himself."[6] DuBose believes that "what is wanted for the life of the Church, and of the world through it," is our "simple and living recognition of a Christ present to our faith and present in our faith." We do not believe in "an absent, past, or future Christ." Instead, it is "in the Church through which as His body our Lord incarnates Himself in all who are in Him."[7] In the church, we are included in the Incarnation and made one with Christ.

The Incarnation was not complete in Christ's earthly life. The "whole process of Incarnation" was "not terminated, it was only begun, in the Ascension of our Lord." The body of Christ's "individual, natural humanity was to grow through all space and time into the all-inclusive body of His corporate, spiritual humanity."[8] The church is the humanity of Christ's "larger incarnation, called His *body*." The church, the "simple presence of Christ to and in Christians," is called the body of Christ because it is "the form and organ of His presence."[9] Of course, the church does not now embody Christ in a perfect way. The sins and imperfections of the members of the church continue to be apparent, and their results are unfortunately visible. Nevertheless, despite present imperfections, the church *is* the body of Christ in the world. In an "already, but not yet" manner, the perfection of Christ's presence is available in the life and sacraments of the church— even though the lived reality of the church has not yet come to embody or represent Christ in a perfect way.

DuBose states that we encounter God's saving presence objectively through the sacraments of baptism and Eucharist. They are the two sacraments of Christ's life, so that baptism is "the sacrament of birth into Him," and the Eucharist is "the sacrament of continuous life in and through Him." They are the "what" and the "how" of our relation "to the living and life-giving Body of Christ."[10] DuBose also holds, "As baptism is the sacrament of our uniting, so the Lord's Supper is that of our continuous and constantly renewed union and communion with God through Christ. They are both sacraments *of life, i.e.* of our union with the life who is Christ. They enable us to say that we are *in Christ*, and that *Christ is in us*."[11] In this regard, he states that "Baptism may be said to correspond to what is now called our justification, and the Holy Communion to our sanctification." He notes that baptism is the "once-for-all identification of us with Christ," and the Eucharist is "the gradual and progressive identification of us with Christ."[12]

DuBose holds the principle that the sacraments really effect what they signify. The Eucharist is "not only a sign of something" and "not a memory or memorial only of Christ"; instead, the Eucharist is "the thing itself of which it is the sign." The Eucharist is "Christ Himself alike the object of our faith and the substance of our life."[13] In this regard, DuBose is entirely consistent with classical sacramental theology: Christ's presence in the sacrament of the Eucharist is "real" because his presence in the church is "real." DuBose states, "if Jesus is in His Church as His living body, and its acts are His living acts, then they cannot but be *real.*" DuBose adds that the real presence of the Eucharist would be "mere magic and superstition" but for "the more general real presence of Christ in His Church."[14]

Christ is likewise present in the world through the life and sacraments of the church. As Christ's human body was "the organ of His natural presence and acts," the church is the "organ of His spiritual presence and activity in the world." Both Christ's human body and the church (including the real presence of the Eucharist) are "part of the general reality and actuality of Christ in Christianity." They are "part of the general system of objective grace, without which there would be no subjective faith or life of Christ in the world."[15]

Accordingly, the Lord's Supper is no "dead formality" which merely *represents* God's presence for our salvation. DuBose explains that the Eucharist stands for and affirms "the objective reality and real presence of *God's part* in our Salvation, the objective grace without which there would not be the subjective faith which is only responsive to and receptive of it." Sacramental language such as the statement in the eucharistic liturgy "this is my body" is not to be understood as merely representing or signifying Christ's body. Instead, "the true instinct and mind of the Church clings, as it has always done, to the living and operative presence of Christ in His Church, and in those acts of the Church which are specifically His own acts."[16] DuBose understands "this is my body" to be a statement about the church as well as the Eucharist.

The Eucharist *is* "God Himself present to perform, and actually performing, His part in our Salvation."[17] Once again, however, the saving process involves both objective gift and subjective realization. Christ is really and objectively present in the sacrament of the Eucharist. Lack of faith does not, therefore, "take Christ out of the Sacrament." Christ is "there, if not for my acceptance, then for my rejection, or at least non-acceptance."[18]

DuBose also states with respect to the sacrament of baptism, "the truth of baptism" is that Christ "who became incarnate for me" does also "become so in me." If the Incarnation did not become a reality in the life of the believer, the truth of the Incarnation would be "only an historical fact, an event of eighteen hundred years ago."[19] "The truth of baptism" is the reality of the Incarnation *in us*, as the truth of the Eucharist is the reality of Christ's real and saving presence in our lives. DuBose states that "in the New Testament, baptism is just as little a mere symbol as Jesus Christ Himself is. As Christ is not an idea but a fact . . . so baptism is actually all that it signifies,— Christ in the individual man, and the man in Christ; and in Christ dead to sin, and alive to God."[20] Baptism *is* what it signifies. Baptism signifies and effects our union with Christ's body for our salvation, making us sharers in his life/death/resurrection experience. The church's sacraments are no mere ritual ceremonies. They are living expressions of Christ's active presence in us for our salvation.

DuBose explains the importance of divine initiative relative to the effectiveness of the sacraments of baptism and Eucharist. But for the activity of Jesus Christ in uniting us "with Himself in union" and sustaining "that union in continuous communion," "no faith of ours makes us, or can make us, in any real and actual sense sons of God and partakers of the divine life."[21] In terms of God's initiative in our regeneration through baptism, DuBose notes, "Baptism is the instrument of 'adoption and grace,' whereby we are 'made children of God.' In regeneration, faith is simply receptive, it is not creative. A man is regenerated *through* not *by* his faith."[22] God's objective gift for our salvation must come first. We can only receive and realize what we have already been given.

The initiative of God's gift for our salvation is objective, but our reception of it is necessarily subjective. DuBose distinguishes objective gift from its subjective realization in his discussion of baptism. DuBose does not compromise the great objective significance of baptism for salvation; baptism is "wholly a *divine* act complete in itself, but to be completed in us only as we receive it." Objectively, baptism is our regeneration. Christ is "wholly given" to every baptized person "in all His death to sin and in all His life to God."[23] Nevertheless, the objective gift of baptismal regeneration is to be subjectively realized through a lifetime of faith.

DuBose stresses this point with respect to the baptism of infants. Objectively, the divine act of regeneration is complete at the baptism of an infant. But that regeneration must be realized subjectively by faith. A baptized infant is "objectively or potentially regenerated" by the act of baptism, but not yet "subjectively or actually" regenerated.[24] At the time of baptism, our regeneration is "already" an objective reality *for* us. It is "not yet" a subjective completed reality *in* us.

DuBose's "already but not yet" understanding of baptismal regeneration is formative for his view of the Christian life that should follow baptism. Once again, theological understanding and experience are closely related for DuBose. Concerning the Christian nurture of the baptized child, he states, "What the child's faith has to accomplish is not to *make* himself son of God, nor to move God by an act contingent upon it to make him so, but simply to accept, to subjectively realize and make good, the fact that God *has made* him, and that he *is* son of God."[25] There is no need for the baptized child to cause or qualify for God's adoption, because that objective reality has been expressed and effected in baptism. But the saving process still needs to be completed through the faith of a lifetime. The process of salvation is therefore deeply related to the life and sacraments of the church. These sacraments objectively signify and effect the gift of salvation, which must be realized subjectively in the personal life of the believer.

The Incarnation is a continuing process that includes the completing of salvation in all humanity. Outwardly and visibly, this process is effected by baptism. "It is baptism by which the Incarnation and all it includes is extended to and made to include us." Baptism expresses the inclusiveness of God's love. When Christ "takes us up by baptism and includes us in the still continuing process of His self-incarnation, He takes us into the fellowship of His still operative death and resurrection."[26] Accordingly, for us, the realization of our baptism is "the substance of Christianity." To realize our baptism is "to bring to reality through faith all God's grace to us in Christ," constituting "an actual and completed death to sin and life to God."[26] "As Luther expresses it in substance, the function of Christian faith is to realize our baptism; it is subjectively appropriating and making good the fact that we *have been* made the sons of God."[28] Thus, DuBose emphasizes that we really encounter Christ's life in and through the church. The completed meaning of this encounter is our salvation.

Baptism signifies the objective beginning of the saving process in our lives, and baptism *is* what it signifies. The church's baptisms are as really Christ's births into individual lives "as His birth of the Virgin was a real birth into humanity." Likewise, "to every man his own baptismal day is at once a true Christmas day and a true birthday, the day of the birth of Christ in him and of his own birth in Christ." The sacrament of baptism embodies Christ's power "to give life to as many as will receive Him" by taking us "into the fellowship and reality of His own risen life."[29] The objective gift of Christ's life in baptism must still be received subjectively through faith for the completing of salvation. It is through Christ's active presence in our lives that we begin, continue, and complete the saving process.

THE CHURCH AS THE COMMUNITY OF SALVATION IN CHRIST

Through the church we receive salvation in Christ, and participate in the saving process. The church is much more than a collection of like-minded people with a common interest in religion. Rather, "as Adam in the New Testament frequently means humanity in Adam or the race, so Christ frequently means humanity in Christ or the Church. There is thus an analogy between our relation to Adam as head of the race and to Christ as head of the Church."[30] We share Christ's salvation in and through the church.

Our union as Christians with Christ and with each other in Christ "constitutes a unity as real as that of our nature with Adam." This real union of Christians "is the true notion of the Church."[31] Indeed, it is through this real union with Christ in the church that we are made sharers and participants in Jesus' sonship, "His own relation with the Father."[32] DuBose explains in *The Gospel in the Gospels* that Jesus is "not only our Christ but our chrism; the precious oil poured out upon His head runs down to the borders of His garment, and anoints His whole mystical person, which is the body of the redeemed and sanctified humanity."[33] The church is Christ's "mystical body," and the continuation of the Incarnation.[34]

DuBose explains that the Incarnation as a "particular fact" was completed in Christ's ascension, but that "generically" the Incarnation "is the Incarnation of God in man, in humanity; and is still in process, not to be completed until Christ is glorified in His mystical body, the Church."[35] Our salvation is to be through the glorification of Christ's mystical body, the church. The "end and consummation" of Christ's work shall be "His glorification in His saints, the redemption of the body of His Church."[36] As Christ "has glorified humanity in His own individual body, so is He to glorify it in the great body of His saints, who are only such as they are in Him and He in them."[37] We the church are the body of Christ in the world. We are thus participants in the "generic" Incarnation, and sharers in the life/death/resurrection experience of Jesus' body.

DuBose points to a radical identification of the church with Christ. He asks, rhetorically, "Why otherwise is the Church, the humanity of His [Christ's] larger incarnation, called His *body*, but that He has united it to Himself in order that in Him it might be sanctified and saved, *just as* He has destroyed sin and been the author of holiness in His natural body, the body of His lesser and more limited incarnation?"[38] Jesus' objective and individual Incarnation was "only as a means and a step to His subjective and generic incarnation" in humanity. This "subjective and generic" Incarnation "is as truly and as really in process and progress in the Church as it was in Him."[39]

The radical identification of Christ and church means that "the Church is as truly *He* as the body of flesh in which He was visibly present on earth."[40] Christ's mission is actually continued by the disciples Jesus commissioned and by the church. He explains that this commission "recognizes the fact that the work of the Church is to be precisely that of Christ Himself, that of reconciliation with God through remission of sin. The sacramental act as well as the general ministry of reconciliation and remission was to be so executed in His name, by His authority, and with His power, that it should be as though God Himself did it by them."[41] This radical identification of Christ with the church therefore concerns not only what the church is, but what the church *does* in terms of the ministry of reconciliation in Christ's name and authority.

We may draw several conclusions from DuBose's ecclesiology. He upholds a radical identification of Christ and the church. The Incarnation continues in the church, making Christ's salvation available. As we participate by faith in the life and sacraments of the church, we continue in the saving process that includes us in Christ's life/death/resurrection experience. Through the church we are made members of Christ's body, and sharers of his salvation.

OUR PARTICIPATION IN SALVATION THROUGH THE CHURCH

DuBose urges that we are to participate in the process of salvation as we share in the life and sacraments of the church. The truths of Christ, the church, and the sacraments "are truths for us only as they are and are to be truths in us."[42] In his chapter "The Christian in Christ" in *The Gospel According to Saint Paul*, based on Romans 6:1–11, DuBose notes that baptism is "a burial with Christ not only into His death but into a fellowship with His dying, and a resurrection with Christ not only into the fact of His life but into the power of His living." Baptism into Christ's death and resurrection "is nothing except as it is also and equally baptism into our own dying and rising with Him."[43] This saving participation is likewise continued through the Eucharist. He states, "as baptism is our admission into, so the Eucharist is our continued participation in the power and fact of Christ's death and resurrection; the means by which they become, or are made, truly *ours*."[44] Sacramental participation is integral to the completion of the saving process.

DuBose emphasizes that the sacraments do not merely signify Christ's life/death/resurrection experience. Through participation in the sacraments we may be effectively included in Christ's victory. In the New Testament, "the truth that baptism constitutes such a real relation between Jesus Christ and us, and between His death and resurrection and ours, is as vital a part of our Salvation as that Jesus Christ Himself was what He was, and suffered and did what He did."[45] Our inclusion in the Incarnation is the "truth that Baptism constitutes." Salvation is thus made available to us. "It is baptism by which the Incarnation and all it includes is extended to and made to include us."[46] We are included in the Incarnation, and Christ's salvation, as we participate in the life and sacraments of the church.

It is noteworthy that the sacraments of baptism and Eucharist are for DuBose "Words of God" that are "conveyances" of Christ himself. They are "expressions to us of what He is to us and what we are in Him," which *are* in themselves and *are* to faith what they mean. These "Words of God" "cannot do less than be."[47] The sacraments objectively *express* and effectively *convey* Christ's presence in particular ways for our salvation. But we must still realize the saving meaning of baptism and Eucharist in our lives by faith. Lack of faith can make the sacraments meaningless to us. DuBose explains, "it is not that our faith puts all its reality into the sacrament *in itself*, but only that our lack of faith takes all realization or actualization of the sacrament *out of us*." Through our faith or lack of it, we "either receive God in Christ or else reject and deny Him in every sacramental act."[48] The saving meaning of the objective gift of Christ in the sacraments of baptism and Eucharist must be subjectively realized in our lives by faith.

The "truth of Baptism" goes beyond the form of the baptismal liturgy itself. Through faith we share the "real relation" between Christ and ourselves that will be our salvation. In this relationship the first objective gift and the initiative are his. Baptism "is not regeneration subjectively realized and completed in the man himself, but it is regeneration objectively made his own and secured to him in Christ by the fact of his being in Christ."[49] DuBose emphasizes that our need for saving participation in Christ would have been very real and compelling, whether or not there were a *rite* of baptism. He states, "If there were no such word and no such rite [as baptism] in existence the fact would still remain that unless Jesus Christ can so take us into union with His person as to make us actual participants in His death and resurrection, His own death and resurrection would have no saving significance or efficacy for us."[50] However, there *is* a rite of baptism in the life of the church by which we may encounter and be included in Christ's life/death/resurrection.

Our saving relationship with Christ, like any living relationship, involves a free mutuality of giving. With respect to the truth of Christ, the church, and the sacraments, "all the life of God in us is nothing except as it is all our own freedom, all our own selves, all our own activity and life in God."[51] Although we cannot be saved without Christ, we have the freedom to reject or fail to receive him. Regeneration for the baptized Christian "is *so* his that it will only be not his by his not believing it to be, and his own failure to make it, his own."[52] He emphasizes that *"we are regenerate"* "in the Church, in Christ, in God." However, "if we do not believe it, it will be nothing *to us.*"[53]

Even if the act of faith precedes baptism, the function of faith *follows* baptism. The function of faith "consists in the realization, not only in the understanding but in the will and the life, of what is freely given to us in Christ." The objective gift of salvation in Christ is given to us freely and unconditionally. "Faith is not the condition of God's giving, but only of our receiving."[54] Our faith is not the prerequisite condition for "what is given in Christ by baptism."

But salvation must still be realized and completed in us subjectively by faith. It is not by some arbitrary or legalistic requirement that faith is the condition for our receiving the saving benefits of baptism. The condition is simply "inherent in the nature of the thing" because "we cannot receive spiritual things without faith, for faith is our reception of spiritual things."[55] It is only with the eyes of faith that we can discern and fully experience the spiritual reality of the church's life and sacraments. Only in faith can we receive or participate in spiritual things for salvation. Of course, we may limit the saving benefit we receive in baptism through our lack of faith.

Objectively, baptism expresses and *is* our life in Christ. It is our inclusion in the Incarnation. Baptism "in itself is what it says—God in Christ to us, and we in Christ to God." In terms of its reality *in itself,* "Baptism is not *only* what *we* see in it or believe in it, *how* we take it or *what* we make it." But *"in us,"* baptism "depends infinitely and eternally upon how we take it or what we make it."[56] We can deny ourselves the gift of salvation by our refusal.

Outwardly, to eyes that lack faith, baptism may seem to be nothing more than a relatively short series of words and some splashing with water. But baptism "is able to be just what *we* are able to make, or to receive, it."[57] If we do not limit baptism by our lack of faith, if we do not subjectively refuse it, baptism will mean our salvation. DuBose draws an analogy between the need for faith to discern and receive the spiritual reality of baptism, and the faith that was needed to discern the human Jesus to be the Christ. He asks, rhetorically, "whether there is any greater discrepancy between the divine meaning and the outward seeming of an act of baptism than there was between the divine reality and the human appearance of that Virgin Birth which gave life to the world. But if we think so little of baptism because there *is* so little in it, is it not possible that there is so little in it because we think so little of it?"[58] Jesus, like baptism, apparently looked "ordinary" to those who did not see with eyes of faith. But their failure to perceive did not in any way diminish his divinity or the objective salvation that he offered. However, their lack of faith or subjective refusal of salvation did limit what *they* received from him. If we were to reject and "make naught" our regeneration in baptism, then "it would no more make baptism not a divine and a divinely efficacious act, than the fact of our Lord's inability to do His mighty works, on account of men's unbelief, made Him not a divine person."[59]

With eyes of faith we can discern and receive the saving benefits of Christ through baptism. Without faith, there would be no saving experience or participation in the life and sacraments of the church. But with faith we may have a saving encounter with Christ through the sacraments. As we receive and participate in Christ's life, his objective gift of salvation will become a subjective reality in our lives. This process is the saving Incarnation, which includes us in Christ's victory. Our salvation is the subjective completion of this process. We share in this saving process as we participate faithfully in the life and sacraments of the church.

THE DISCERNMENT OF TRUTH IN THE COMMUNITY OF THE CHURCH

Experience, Community, and Discernment

One of the most significant and interesting aspects of DuBose's ecclesiology is his understanding of the role of the church community in the discernment of truth. This aspect of his theology has direct implications for pastoral life as the church faces theological controversies, disagreements, and confusions. The church's role in the discernment of truth can be continually tested at all levels of ecclesial experience, ranging from a congregational committee to a diocesan synod or convention to a bilateral dialogue of denominations to a Christian ecumenical council.

DuBose holds that the reality of truth can be discerned through human experience and that the community of faith is needed to receive and discern the fullness of truth. This represents a continuation and development of his emphasis on the role of human experience in the saving process.

"God makes spiritual truth for mankind pass through the spiritual experience of mankind and by proving itself true for all to become the truth of all."[60] Spiritual truth must "ring true" to our experience; it must really *save* us. Therefore, "a gospel for us must be a gospel of spiritual and moral freedom, of liberty to be or to become our true and complete selves; it must remove the bond of blindness from the eye, of deafness from the ear, of ignorance from the mind, of weakness from the will, of sin from the soul and of death from the life."[61] DuBose thus provides a vivid expression of the relationship between spiritual truth and human experience. The truth of the Gospel is a real truth that we can discern and experience in our lives.

In terms of our recognition of spiritual truth through experience, DuBose finds that "the truth of Christ is a matter of ourselves as well as of God." He explains, "The authority of the church, the authority of the Scriptures, the authority of our Lord, the authority of God, are all a very great deal along with the authority of a really universal human experience. . . . Without the latter it would be impossible that all the former should possess for us any weight or value."[62] Although DuBose recognizes the importance of church tradition, he also upholds the importance of our experience in the life of faith and the discernment of truth. There is much more to participation in spiritual truth than our acceptance of received tradition on the basis of church authority. Our participation in the truths of faith is not *just* conceptual. For example, the theological statement "Jesus saves" must also be a living reality in our personal experience as we participate and continue in the saving process.

DuBose's identification of the importance of "universal human experience" underscores his assumption that the community of faith is needed to receive and discern the fullness of truth. He states that "the common or universal spiritual consciousness and experience of the whole Christian church is the only test of what Christianity is."[63] Concerning the verdict of a church council, he holds that "it can only be ascertained that the verdict is true, and will stand by a long and silent process through which the decision is referred back to the church again to say whether it has correctly expressed itself through its council. If the church thus accepts the council as its voice, by that fact it imparts to it an authority which is its own and not that of the council."[64] Even the ultimate authority of a church council is subject to reception of the truth by the whole church. For DuBose, the doctrines of faith and the church's lived experience of faith must not be divorced from each other.

The fullness of spiritual truth is known and experienced in the community of the church, although each of us must also experience the truth personally. Nevertheless, despite the importance of individual experience, the emphasis of DuBose's approach is definitely on the experience and "mind" of the church as a whole. In view of the importance of corporate experience and theological reflection in the church, there is necessarily a limited degree of originality in the work of any individual Christian theologian. DuBose urges that "the greatest genius who has risen to recognition as a Christian theologian has been independent of the common thought or of the common results of thought in the church only to the extent of some infinitesimal addition of his own to the common store of its knowledge and doctrine."[65] This observation is especially interesting since DuBose has been described as the "most original and creative thinker" in the history of the Episcopal Church.[66]

Our experiences of spiritual truth must take place in the context of Christian tradition. For Christian theology, "as in every other department of human experience and knowledge no individual who really adds to or advances it begins at the beginning but only at the end of an already long and large accumulation of tested, verified and accepted truth which it is ignorance and folly to ignore and to which no one who ignores it can possibly have anything to add."[67] Our evaluation of spiritual truth takes place in the context of Christian community, including not only present community but also the "verified and accepted truth" of the Christian community that has preceded us. DuBose states that "there is such a thing as a catholic mind; there are already results that have finally approved themselves and will nevermore be shaken." He notes that these theological "results" reflect the "efforts, errors and corrections of the past and the confirmations, agreements and certitudes that have been attained through them."[68]

\DuBose likewise points out that the fullness of spiritual truth is more than any individual can fathom. This is because "a complete and all-sided faith or life is not promised or given to any individual man, and no single man even with the aid of the Scriptures holds such except as the gift to him in whole or for the most part of the common thought and knowledge of the Church." He warns that "the very elevation and intensity of individual attention and experience in one direction withdraws it from other directions of quite equal truth and importance."[69] He clearly identifies the necessary limitation and potential danger of any theological perspective in isolation.

In the context of controversy, for example, an ardent defender of Jesus' full divinity may neglect to defend Jesus' full humanity with equal clarity—or vice versa. With respect to the Council of Ephesus (431) and its controversy over Nestorianism, DuBose states, "Cyril is singularly clear and sound in detecting the logical tendencies and dangers of the opposite side, but of the possibility of a contribution of truth from that direction such as was to be recognized and accepted in the Council of Chalcedon, he and his party seem as yet to have caught no inkling."[70] The Council of Ephesus thus provides an instance in which one side may fail to acknowledge the partial truths in the other side. One danger in upholding one side too strongly in a controversy is the possibility of not acknowledging that one's own side represents partial truths and potential weaknesses.

The danger of upholding a position too strongly does not mean that disagreement should be avoided. On the contrary, it is only in the context of sharing different perspectives within the community that the paradoxes and inconsistencies of spiritual truth can be comprehended. But this sharing must be done with a view to the larger comprehension and discernment of the church, which includes and surpasses individual perspectives. DuBose notes that "only such a complex resultant of the operation of many minds and lives as we have in the Scriptures or in the church can combine the whole truth or express the sum of Christian experience."[71] He uses a historical example to illustrate:

> at the end of the fourth century no theology could have originated within the church which did not intend to hold, and believe itself to hold, the reality of both the divinity and the humanity in a real incarnation. We only mean to illustrate the fact that nothing short of a catholic doctrine, a doctrine of the mind of the church as a whole, could be broad enough and comprehensive enough to embrace at once on all its sides the totality of the truth of Jesus Christ, and that prior to such a doctrine no one theologian did or could so hold the whole truth as not unconsciously to deny or mutilate some one part in the supposed interest of some other part.[72]

In this regard, he shows sensitivity to both sides or emphases concerning the church's christological doctrine, and he expresses the extreme difficulty involved in any individual attempt to make a "comprehensive" statement.

DuBose likewise found that the limitations of individual experience and theological perspective were as real in his day as they were in the fourth century. He urges that "no one mind can simultaneously and equally appreciate all that is involved in the whole truth of the incarnation."[73] There is a fundamental humility in DuBose's approach that is very significant for all who engage in theological reflection. No one perspective or theological camp is comprehensive enough to have all the answers, and the truth is best known in the church as a variety of different theological perspectives come together and are tested. Even if the truth of a particular perspective is incomplete, it may still be valuable to the extent that it is true. The "Gospel of Jesus Christ is so true and so living in every part that he who truly possesses and truly uses any broken fragment of it may find in that fragment something—just so much—of gospel for his soul and of salvation for his life."[74]

DuBose's suspicion of the comprehensiveness of theological factions and camps is also visible in his wariness concerning "all the modern *isms*" of Christianity that "are but broken fragments of the Truth that is One and is ever the Same." With respect to the "isms," he warns that although "our sects and our parties live by the truth that is in them and that is vital in them, they are but too apt to live also in a deadly competition with other truths as true as they, and so in fatal detriment to the whole and the wholeness of truth."[75]

Although he does not specify the identity of any of the "isms," his warning seems to apply equally to the pitfalls of extreme "liberalism" and "traditionalism" in the life of the church. DuBose's work offers to the position of extreme traditionalism a "liberal reminder" that "the Holy Spirit is still active in the church and in the people's lives and that God's revelation is continuous, not static." Similarly, his work offers to the position of extreme liberalism a "catholic reminder" that "today's truth is continuous with the truth already received by the church."[76] He emphatically sought to avoid confusing "broken fragments of the Truth" (as held by any side or "ism") with the comprehensive truth of the church.

DuBose emphasizes that the church should not be intimidated by the potential error contained in the various expressions and perspectives that are offered as truths of faith. Instead, the church should stand ready to hear, test, and prove what is presented as truth. He states, "The best expulsion of error is through the freedom permitted to it of self-exposure. Our end in view is not the licensing of error, but the ultimate best, if not only, method of eliminating error by suffering it to meet and be overcome by truth."[77] He warns against "the impossibility of extinguishing error by legislation or banishing it by exclusion, or of getting rid of it in any other way than by meeting and overcoming it with the truth." There is "no surer way" to propagate error "than to prosecute, suppress and exclude liberty." Accordingly, the church should "not be afraid to keep herself in perpetual question by her own children." The church has nothing to fear from the truth, wherever the truth may be found. The church should thus "have all the benefit" of the truth in what is said, as the church should "meet and answer" any error with the truth.[78] The church's willingness to hear out divergent viewpoints implies no reluctance to distinguish truth from error.

DuBose holds that the "breadth and freedom of Christian experience and experiment" by which "the Church itself, as a whole, formulated its truth and shaped its life in the beginning" must also be allowed to the members of the church as they make the truth and life of Christianity their "individual and personal own." He warns, "if you say that one shall make no mistakes, shall fall into no errors, then you say that he shall not know the truth for himself nor live a life that is his own." Therefore, "if there is no freedom of error within the Church, then there is no freedom of truth."[79] The church has no reason to fear the openness that is needed to hear and discern truth. The living truth will be sufficient to overcome the dangers of error and falsity, so long as the truth is allowed to *be* a living truth and encounter the questions that face the church.

For DuBose, the exercise of freedom by a person or by the church is more than mere flexibility to choose between options or preferences. This freedom is ultimately the capacity to choose and complete a living identity and way of being. In soteriological terms, personal freedom is necessary for participating in the saving process and subjectively receiving salvation. The fulfilment of Christian formation in personal life and identity requires freedom. The church also must have freedom to actualize its objective identity as the body of Christ. Freedom (even the freedom to err) is at the heart of the process by which Christian identity is to be personally and subjectively realized in our lives and in the church.

The Church as an Open Forum for Discernment

DuBose's assumption concerning the role of the church community led to his position that the life of the church should be an open forum in which conflicting perspectives and tendencies can be worked out. He urges that "extremes will reconcile themselves, or will work themselves out, lose their sting, and leave their contribution if recognized and recognizing their common right within the Church."[80] As there is "a truth of the Scripture to be known and a mind of the Church to be understood and shared," there is a unity in diversity in which "we shall gratefully acknowledge one another's contributions of truth, whatever they may be; and we shall not content ourselves with anathematizing one another's shortcomings or errors."[81] DuBose points beyond a spirit of mere partisanship in the church's life and controversies. He states in his preface to *The Gospel in the Gospels*, "So let us agree to disagree, if conscientiously we must, in all our manifold differences; and, bringing all our differences together, let us see if they are not wiser than we, and if they cannot and will not of themselves find agreement in a unity that is higher and vaster than we."[82] The comprehensive truth can be revealed as differing viewpoints are encountered and tested in the church. He notes that "truth is only made known and indeed only knows itself in conflict with error." He describes the "collective mind of the church which sooner or later excludes what is spiritually false and includes what is spiritually true."[83] Truth and distortion will eventually "prove themselves" to be what they are in the life and experience of the church.

In light of this process for discerning the truth through the whole life of the church, we need not regard spiritual truth as fragile. J. O. F. Murray notes in his study of DuBose that he "strove earnestly to reassure the authorities of the Church who were trembling for the safety of the Ark of God."[84] DuBose sought to inspire such "trembling authorities" "with his own conviction that the truth, which won consent in the past after the freest discussion, has nothing to fear from the unrestrained criticism of the present. It can safely be trusted to defend itself, if the field is left open."[85] DuBose holds that the truth of the Scriptures and the mind of the church will each "take care of itself as against the infinite errors and vagaries of individual thinkers and writers."[86] While we should be concerned to express spiritual truth with the utmost accuracy, we should not be insecure about the possibility of error. If we refuse to accept the risk of some error, we will be unable to attempt new articulations of the truth we have experienced. DuBose states, "The ultimate aim of each one of us should be not to save ourselves from error but to advance the truth. We may safely rely upon it that our truth will in the end be accepted and our error corrected. If I had been too much afraid of going wrong I should have made no progress in growing right. . . ."[87] The church is to provide an open forum to discern truth and correct error in the midst of various opinions and expressions.

DuBose does not provide step-by-step suggestions for the implementation of an open forum in the church. His introductory chapter to *The Reason of Life*, titled "Principles of Unity," describes the practical and theological importance of Christian unity and offers goals and principles for that unity. However, he admits that "the present volume has no practical solutions to offer." Instead, it "would only prepare and propose the spirit and temper" in which these issues concerning Christian unity "should be undertaken and may be solved."[88] Nevertheless, his support for any reasonable effort to draw together theology and the people of the church can be inferred from his prolific theological writings and his emphasis on experience and personal participation in the saving process. He believed in theology and in the life of the church, and in their significance for each other.

Furthermore, the church *as a whole* should provide venues and occasions for testing theological perspectives in an open forum. DuBose did not restrict his audience to professional theologians or theological specialists. For example, *Turning Points in My Life* includes "an address upon The Theology of the Child, read the day after the [1911 DuBose] reunion by request of a Sunday School Conference which succeeded it."[89] Similarly, a letter from DuBose commending *The Trinity Course of Church Instruction* by Bishop C. M. Beckwith was published in the introductory portion of that book. In addition to praising Beckwith's "ideas and methods of catechetical instruction," DuBose notes that "we have practically ceased too much to be a teaching Church, and consequently have lost too much our sanctifying and saving power."[90] He sought to be a theologian for the whole church, and he sought for the whole church to provide an open forum for discerning theological truth.

In providing an open forum, the church must seek to rediscover the ancient truths of Christian faith in light of the experiences, needs, and contexts of the present. In this regard, the church's life and discernment may be understood in liberal catholic terms. DuBose urges that the truth of the Scripture and the mind of the church "are not dead but live things." Since they are "always alive," they are also "always in question" and "under the necessity of being always our truth, and not merely that of other thinkers and of another age."[91] He also states in a preface to a book by William Law, "We want, after all, not William Law, but what William Law stands for, or stood for in his day. Essentially that is the same thing then and now; but it needs to be stood for now as well as then. A living truth wants living, and not only dead, witnesses."[92] The truth of the church, the truth of Christian tradition—like the truth of any Christian theologian—must be rediscovered in the present moment and expressed through "living witnesses."

DuBose certainly upholds the authority of church tradition, noting that "the Church must stand for the accumulation and organization of that which is common, that which has passed into consent and agreement, has become *res adjudicata*, as over against the infinite diversities and vagaries of individual Christians." However, "on the other hand," the church must likewise remember that "catholic truth or consent" was itself "the outcome or resultant of only the very utmost diversity, which means freedom of thought and experience at the first." Accordingly, "the Church that does not hold itself and keep itself open to conviction and correction from within itself is not a living Church." As "catholic truth was formulated only over against and in conflict with every possible kindred error," so "its life consists still in its being the truth" and "its continued living depends upon its continuous power to affirm and maintain itself against every form of opposing error." DuBose warns that if catholicity ever "becomes only a victory of the past, no longer needing, and therefore by consequence losing its power, to defend and maintain itself in the present, in that moment it begins to become a mere fossil or fetich." The truth of faith is alive, not stagnant, and we are to discern, engage, and share its living reality. "Dogma must not only have approved itself and won consent; it must continue to approve itself and be able to retain consent."[93]

DuBose states in the essay "Christian Defense" that "the delicacy, the dexterity and exactness with which Christianity at the first defined and defended itself against every conceivable false conception and false expression" was unsurpassed. However, he also warns that "the time has come" when Christianity must "recall and renew its ancient power of self-comprehension and its ancient skill of self-presentation, if it would hold its own in the arena of the present." This thesis is at the heart of DuBose's liberal catholicism and his ecclesiology. He strongly urges that "it will not suffice" for Christianity "to have been once proved and approved; it must be capable of always anew proving and approving itself to the questionings of each new age."[94] The ancient saving truth of Christianity must be discovered anew in each context of the church and articulated as living witness.

Similarly, in *High Priesthood and Sacrifice*, DuBose strongly urges that "the Hebrew phrases and terms of priesthood and sacrifice, and the Greek or Gentile application of them to the Cross of Christ" are not "waxed old and ready to vanish away."[95] But for these phrases and terms to be "as living today" as they were before, "we must cease to treat the phraseology, the forms, definitions, and dogmas of Christianity as sacred relics, too sacred to be handled. We must take them out of their napkins, strip them of their cerements, and turn them into current coin. We must let them do business in the life that is living now, and take part in the thought and feeling and activity of the men of the world of to-day."[96] He sought to "vindicate" the "eternal, unchangeable truth and validity" of "those most ancient forms or figures of priesthood, high priesthood, and sacrifice" by "handling them freely, by translating them as completely as I can into the current terms of our own thought and speech and life."[97] He sought to rediscover the ancient truths of faith and express them in light of current language and experience, thus converting the ancient truths into "current coin."

ᵗ The truths of faith must be experienced and known for our salvation today. It is the *truth* of the truths of faith that gives them authority, not the authority of the church that gives them truth. DuBose states in "Liberty and Authority in Christian Truth," "If we have the truth wrapped up in a napkin as a sacred deposit handed down from the past, if we hold it now as the decision of a council or the letter of a Creed and not by the continuous self-demonstration of its truth in itself and its meaning and necessity to us, then indeed may our dead or dormant catholicity be afraid of the much alive and wide-awake heresies that confront it as in the earliest days."[98] On the contrary, he warns, "nothing but the life and the living thought that shaped the decisions and wrought the creeds can maintain the decisions or defend the creeds now."[99] DuBose's statements of method and purpose reveal the essence of his liberal catholic approach to theology, which strongly upholds the continuity of catholic truth while warning that the truth must constantly be experienced anew. He notes, "the fact will always remain that we receive our Christianity through the Scriptures and the Church, and that these are the tribunal of final resort for determining what Christianity is."[100] But he also urges that the continuity of truth must be rediscovered again and again, "liberally," in terms of new forms, contexts, needs, and expressions.

DuBose was open and welcoming to the use of contemporary insights and methods for testing and discerning truth. He was not afraid of the scientific method or biblical criticism. At the end of his major section "The Gospel of the Earthly Life or the Common Humanity" in *The Gospel in the Gospels*, he notes that he endeavored to make "full proof and use of the truth, or aspects of the truth, which modern knowledge, and modern methods of knowledge, have revealed or opened up to us in the unchanged and unchangeable Gospel." But he also concludes that "the new light does not change our old Gospel."[101]

Similarly, in *The Gospel According to Saint Paul*, DuBose reflects his belief in the continuity of the Gospel as known through the changing forms and understandings of his day: "We ourselves within a generation have undergone revolutions in our traditional beliefs of historical truth and natural fact which we once thought part of our religious faith, and have made for ourselves the oft-repeated discovery that the removal of the things that are shaken does not involve the change of those that may not be shaken. It is impossible but that St. Paul had his traditional beliefs that were subject to change, and that he used them in expression and illustration of the things that cannot change."[102] The "old Gospel" must be known in new forms; the cause of the Gospel is ultimately furthered by whatever reveals the truth.

The church should be unafraid to discern the truth, or to discover the truth in new forms and expressions, or to accept what is truly discerned by others outside the church.

The truth may be known through the sifting, weighing, and correcting of spiritual knowledge and experience in the life of the church. DuBose thus outlines a process of discernment that involves an interplay of experience with theological reflection and expression. As this dynamic interplay unfolds, neither experience nor theological reflection and expression can be allowed to exclude the other. This involves "a process by which the experience gradually fits and adjusts itself to the truth and the truth gradually approves and proves itself to the experience; and so the two become one in a union from which there is afterward no possible divorce."[103] Of course, the church's process of discerning spiritual truth must continue. In this mortal life there is always more of God that surpasses our present understanding. For example, DuBose notes that christology will "never be complete," but "there is a truth in it of which while it is greater than our knowledge we may yet know more and more."[104]

Even if the truths of our individual perspectives and positions are limited and partial, we can find in the church the possibility of sharing in a truth and a comprehension of truth that is larger than ourselves in isolation. Our own experiences and reflections can be "fitted and adjusted" relative to the experiences and reflections of others, including those who have gone before us in the Christian faith.

We also can share our experiences and reflections in ways that may influence the "fitting and adjusting" of the church's process of discernment. Thus there may be a dynamic interplay and mutual correction between individual and corporate experience, as well as a similar dialectical relationship between experience and tradition in the life of the church. Through it all, we may participate in the process of discerning spiritual truth most fully as we share and contend and listen together in the community of the church. The "truth of Christ" is known in the body of Christ, the church.

THE UNITY AND ECUMENICITY OF THE CHURCH

DuBose's ecclesiology was a theology of church unity. This ecumenical emphasis was especially true during the last years of his life, as evidenced by his many contributions to the ecumenical journal the *Constructive Quarterly* and other writings. The nineteenth and early twentieth centuries were a time of significant ecumenical initiatives in the Episcopal

Church and the Anglican Communion; these initiatives clearly influenced DuBose.

DuBose was also influenced powerfully by the optimistic and progressive spirit of his era. In 1911 he perceived that "we are moving now upon a very flood tide of opportunity. The thought of the world is upon and the demand of the time is for unity. We have entered upon an era of reconciliation and cooperation."[105] Although DuBose recognized that abuses were still present in the world, he believed that the death knell had been struck for "all inequitable inequalities, and inevitable consequent strife," including the "clash of capital and labor, of organized and free employment, of privilege and equality, of special and general interests." Similarly, DuBose noted in 1911 that the general "raising of the question of arbitration and peace" was "the surest prognostic of a progressive approximation to its solution such as will be at least the diminution and amelioration if not the actual extinction of war."[106]

Unfortunately, the years that followed this statement did not bring a diminution and amelioration of war. DuBose's association with such ideas may have damaged his credibility with some people in light of the carnage and disillusionment of World War I, which soon followed. Nevertheless, these sentiments certainly reveal the extent of personal transformation experienced in his lifetime by this graduate of The Citadel and former officer in the Confederate Army. From this personal change we can infer DuBose's own participation in the saving process through his lifetime experience of Christian faith.

DuBose accorded church unity the highest priority for action. He noted in his 1906 essay "Liberty and Authority in Christian Truth" that "agreement in truth and unity in life, at-one-ment with God and with one another, are the end and the task of Christianity."[107] By 1911, he believed that "all the spirits and signs of the time" were turned "in the direction of unity," and that Christian unity was "the one problem and task of the age."[108] In 1918, he identified "the task of religious reconstruction" as the "most essential condition of the general world reconstruction now impending."[109]

DuBose's emphasis on the unity of the church certainly anticipates the development of the ecumenical movement that was to engage many Christian denominations and theologians in the twentieth century. Christian unity is "of the essence of Christianity."[110] He urges that "to be Christians we must not only be all in Christ, but we must be in all Christ," who is "all Christianity as well as each Christian," and "all Humanity."[111] Christianity and unity "are identical things," so "we cannot sacrifice or surrender the one and preserve or possess the other."[112]

For DuBose, the church, which is "the Community and Communion of the Saints, the Body of Christ, the Organ of the Holy Ghost," is also "the unity of Christians with Christ, and with one another in Christ."[113] The church is "in the highest sense the sacrament of unity."[114] The "Kingdom of God is nothing if it is not organized and ordered unity," and the "Church of God is no living thing if it is not something more than human organization— the divine organism and organ of unity human and divine."[115] The church "may be defined as organized unity, or as unity incarnate." He describes the unity of the church in imperative terms, noting that "God in Christ recognizes no oneness with Him that is not oneness of all in Him with one another."[116]

With respect to the four "notes" of the church ("one," "holy," "catholic," and "apostolic") as stated in the Nicene Creed, DuBose urges that the "first note," unity, is "the one all-sufficient note." He explains, for example, that "it is not being holy that makes us one with God, one in ourselves, or one with one another: it is the being one that makes us holy, that is our holiness." The church's "one mark of unity includes and covers all the others, of holiness, universality and perpetuity."[117] Church unity is thus at the heart of DuBose's ecclesiology. As the church continues the Incarnation, the unity of the church is our unity in Christ who prayed that those who believe in him "may all be one."

DuBose did not offer "practical solutions" for the obstacles to Christian unity. But he did present four principles in *The Reason of Life* as a "first step" toward the realization of Christian unity: (1) unity is to be accepted by all as "the principle and essence of Christianity," and "the duty of every Christian"; (2) each "separate name or body of Christians" is to "realize and emphasize as much as possible what it has in common with the one whole Church of Christ, and efface as far as possible all divisive and individual or party elements, badges, or expressions"; (3) differences that are "felt to be vital or important" are to be "held in trust for all and not arrogated as the possession of a few or a part"; and (4) "Christian intercourse, interchange, and cooperation" are to be encouraged as much as possible, and in all conferences there is to be "the utmost of plain-speaking with as much as possible of mutual understanding and charity," so that "all the truth" is "spoken as each sees it," but the truth is spoken "in all the love of Christ."[118]

DuBose encourages the inclusion of diversity in the church rather than demanding "an impossible uniformity." Christian unity is "so essential and so necessary a thing" that "the limits of uniformity must be stretched to their utmost in the interest of even the lowest practicable unity."[119] But his ecumenical theology calls for much more than mere toleration of differences. In the context of an essay concerning the two "extremes" of Evangelical and Catholic, he states, "not for any particular Church, but for Christianity as a whole, there has to be, not alone a consent 'to live and let live,' but a deeper understanding, a truer union, and a more real sense of oneness between Evangelical and Catholic." Furthermore, he finds this principle to be true not only for the Church of England, but for "the whole Church and Christianity of our time, and possibly of all time." There is much more at stake than benign toleration of opposing tendencies. He explains that "each side needs all the true emphasis of the other for more than correction—for completion of itself."[120] We need each other in the church—despite our differences, indeed, *because* of our differences—for mutual completion.

It is possible to refine our understanding of DuBose's open forum in light of his passionate commitment to church unity. The open forum for DuBose is not just an expression of open-mindedness and willingness to evaluate all positions fairly. It *is* that, but it is much more. We could perhaps find a fair and open forum in, for example, a debating society or a good radio talk show. But for DuBose, the true meaning of the open forum is only understandable in terms of commitment to Christian unity.

DuBose points to our need for the church as a whole to provide a place and a way for the unfolding of a comprehensive theology. The church is "divinely organized and constituted Unity" in which "by free interrelation and interaction different points of view, impressions, emphases, perspectives, and so theories, doctrines, systems, etc., may correct, supplement, and complete one another and bring all to the essential and sufficient unity that not only belongs to them but can come only through their all-sided contributions."[121] It is because we are incomplete, limited, and fallible in and of ourselves that we need each other for mutual correction and completion. As our "spirit, attitude, and policy" in the church serve "to bring together, compare, and contribute to the common good of the One End, the End of Oneness," the "differences that do not eliminate themselves will be turned into the higher service of deepening, broadening, and heightening the resultant Unity."[122] The ultimate answer to our differences is rooted in the unity we share in Christ, and our commitment to it. That life and commitment provide the basis for the open forum in the church. Without the synthesis that can come from the open forum, the truth of each side and even the truth of the church can be "fragmentary." The church is therefore not only the *place* of unity, but the *way* of unity, providing both venue and context for working out differences and fragmentary truths.

Without the spirit of unity, we may encounter the threat of sectarianism. DuBose finds that the evil of sects in Christianity "is expressed in the word itself: they are organized and isolated differences and diversities."[123] He characteristically identifies the loss *to the church as a whole* that is represented by sectarianism: "Their partial and emphasized good is withdrawn from communication to and influence upon others; their deficiencies, ignorances or errors are removed from supplementing or correction by others."[124] The church is thus deprived by sectarianism that isolates its followers from making their contribution to the open forum of the wider church. And the followers of a sect who are isolated from the open forum of the church are likewise deprived of what they could receive from the wider church for correction and completion. Separation, isolation, or schism of members of the church from one another is therefore a great loss to the church, and all the members who are deprived of each other.

In contrast, DuBose holds, with "that Oneness in Christ which is the essence and definition of Christianity," our differences "would quickly melt down into not merely pardonable or permissible but even contributory and completive diversities."[125] In short, the working out of extremes and differences is not about our trying to fit together the broken pieces of the church into a tolerable composite. It is our unity in Christ and with one another in Christ that is the only ultimate basis for resolving differences in the church. He explains, "there is no common or universal oneness with God that does not abolish between those who share it, I will not say all differences among themselves, but at any rate all differences that deny, contradict, defeat or hinder their oneness together in Him."[126] Our unity in Christ is the only basis for reunion of the denominations in the church and for resolution of our differences.

The culmination of DuBose's system of theology is his ecclesiology. Our salvation is to be received and *lived* in the church. Furthermore, DuBose's ecclesiology culminates in his ecumenical theology. We are to be one in Christ and one with each other in Christ through the unity of the church. Our ecumenism is not merely toleration or open-mindedness, but a recognition that we *need* each other for mutual correction and completion in the unity of the church that saves us. This shared unity in Christ is the only real basis for resolving our differences. It is likewise the most effective means for us to participate in the process of salvation through the life and sacraments of the church. In this way the objective gift of salvation may be subjectively realized in us and our community.

CHAPTER 6

Life, Movement, and Being

THE PRINCIPLE OF SYNTHESIS IN DUBOSE'S THEOLOGY

The Convergence of DuBose's Systematic Themes

DuBose's theology is tightly interwoven, and the various aspects of his theological work are formative for each other. His work is intricately interconnected in terms of the systematic areas identified in this study. For this reason, his theology presents a challenge for any attempt to focus on a particular area to the temporary exclusion of others. The unity of DuBose's theology is best understood as a systematic analysis of the saving process. The Incarnation is to be continued and completed in us, as we receive the objective gift of salvation. This takes place by the active working of the Spirit who makes salvation available in our lives and in the church. Pneumatology is therefore the unifying principle in DuBose's theology. By the Spirit, the objective gift of salvation in Christ may be subjectively fulfilled, leading to our at-one-ment with God.

DuBose emphasizes the role of experience in the saving process and in theological reflection. Salvation is to become actual in our lives through the completing of the saving process. Christ humanly lived and completed the way of salvation. He reveals the way for us to complete the saving process by grace through faith and obedience. We may understand and experience the saving process as the way of the cross, which Christ completed and fulfilled in his life/death/resurrection. This saving experience is realized in us as we freely participate in it.

Salvation is the expression and gift of God's love. Salvation is a matter of life or death. The life that is available for us in Christ is real. DuBose's christology is therefore a christology of salvation. For DuBose, all true christology is soteriological. A "Christ" who did not or could not save us would be, perhaps, a metaphysical curiosity or a topic of interesting discussion. But such a "Christ" would be no true Christ. Christology expresses the truth of Christ who saves, as soteriology expresses the truth of how we are saved in Christ.

The saving process in which we participate is also real. Salvation in Christ is available to us in our human experience, especially in the life and sacraments of the church. The church expresses and makes available the reality of salvation by extending the Incarnation outwardly and visibly in time and space. Christology and soteriology are formative for ecclesiology. The reality of salvation in Christ is formative for the living reality that the church is to be in our world. A "church" that was not a means of salvation would be no true church. Anything in the church that does not serve our salvation is a matter of indifference at best, and dangerous at worst.

The reality of life in the church is also formative for our understanding of christology and soteriology. If an understanding of Christ and salvation does not "ring true" in the lived experience of the church, if it hinders or does not advance the interests of salvation in Christ, it must be reconsidered in light of the experience of the church. Ecclesiology—the lived experience of the church and reflection upon that experience—is formative for christology and soteriology. In this way, ecclesiology provides a fundamental criterion for judgment and discernment. A doctrine or practice of the church that proves to hinder salvation must not be tolerated.

DuBose's emphasis on the reality of salvation reflects his strong emphasis on the role of human experience in the process of salvation and in theological reflection. His own theology was deeply rooted in his entire life experience, especially the "turning points" in his life that reflected his participation in the saving process. His systematic theology integrated his personal journey of faith and human experience with his own appropriation and creative rediscovery of the Christian tradition.

Throughout the system and process of DuBose's theology it is the Holy Spirit that gives power for salvation. The objective gift of salvation in Christ is made present and available to us by the Spirit. The Spirit has been and continues to be active in the saving process of the Incarnation. DuBose notes that the Spirit "prepared the Virgin Mary's faith as well as her womb; and her womb only through her faith."[1] It is likewise the Spirit who "preveniently" prepares us for our subjective completion of the saving process. The Spirit enables and empowers our "yes" of faith by which we freely participate in the process of salvation. Furthermore, it is by the Spirit's activity in the church that we experience Christ "really present" in the church, are included in the saving process of the Incarnation, and participate in the church's life and sacraments. Jesus lived and completed the way of salvation by the Spirit. By the Spirit we may share Jesus' way of holiness and righteousness.

The Spirit is also the principle of unity underlying the ecumenical imperative of DuBose's theology. The content of Christian faith and the work of God are to be understood in light of the mission of the Holy Spirit. The Spirit is the unifying reality in the economy of salvation and the principle of unity in DuBose's soteriological theology. It is by the Spirit that christology and ecclesiology are soteriological. It is by the Spirit that soteriology is *real* and available to us.

The Life, Movement, and Being of the Saving Process

At times DuBose describes the saving process in terms of the statement in Acts 17:28 that in God "we live and move and have our being." We live and move and have our being "only by and in God Himself," only through Christ's "own immediate presence and action in us."[2] This statement is also the basis for the title of my study of DuBose because it epitomizes his theology of the process of salvation, by which we share Christ's life and move to actual completion of the saving process in our own lives. DuBose notes that "faith, hope, love are principles of never ending movement, action, progress."[3] Life is "inseparable and indistinguishable from its movement."[4]

We "move" in the path of life as we participate in the completing of the saving process. We "move" in the saving process as the already completed salvation in Christ becomes increasingly complete in our own lives. This saving process is made possible for us by the Spirit, who makes Christ present for our salvation in our lives and in the church. If we obey the "motions" of God's Spirit, and "take up the true attitude toward our sin, and toward His love and grace and holiness, then He will be faithful and righteous on His part to more than meet our least movement toward Him." "Indeed," DuBose adds, "any movement on our part is already His motion in us."[5] Our "movement" in the saving process reflects God's loving initiative in our lives.

It is for us and for our salvation that Christ is present by the Spirit in our lives and in the church. Even though we have not yet completed this saving process, our participation and movement in it is the way of our salvation. It is our way of mutual fulfilment in love with the "being" of God, so that God lives in us and we live in God. This way of "movement, action, progress" is the way of our salvation in and through "faith, hope, love." It is also the heart of DuBose's system of theology.

Living, moving, and having our being in God require our human experience and participation in the saving process. We cannot "live and move and have our being without God, apart from our personal knowledge of Him and of His personal interest and influence in us." The saving process calls for our life in God and God in our life. DuBose describes humanity in terms of the three stages of natural, moral, and spiritual. The "essential characteristic" of the spiritual third stage is "not the immanent physical fact that in God we live and move and have our being, but the transcendent spiritual fact that, consciously, freely, personally, we are living, moving, having and exercising our being in God." This means that God is "as personally in us as we are in Him for life, that our life is as truly His as His is ours."[6] Christ thus reveals "the divinity of our humanity, a divinity potential only in the beginning, and consisting in a natural relation and in a capacity for personal union, but in the end, as in Him, perfected into a personal oneness with God; in Whom, and of ourselves, we now indeed do consciously, freely, and literally 'live and move and have our being. . . .'"[7] Salvation is a reality for us as we "consciously, freely, and literally" live and move and have our being in God.

DuBose acknowledges that the statement "in Him we live and move and have our being" is "a presupposition of religion" as "the expression of a mere immanent or natural fact" that "God is the underlying and containing cause or condition of all that is." But this statement "only becomes religion" through "spiritual and moral consciousness, acceptance, and experience" whereby "the mere natural fact passes on up and transmutes itself into personal act—that is, as we ourselves in our nature, and not only our nature in us, are personally living and moving, finding, possessing, and exercising our whole being, in God."[8] That we may live and move and have our being in God describes the lived reality of our progressive personal sanctification in Christ by faith through the Spirit in our lives and in the church. As we participate in the saving process, our life, movement, and being in God increasingly become for us a personal fact of our experience. This lived reality also epitomizes the way, the meaning, and the end of DuBose's systematic theology of salvation.

APPLICATION OF DUBOSE'S THEOLOGY

DuBose's theology can remedy the disjunction that tends to exist between the pastoral life of the church and serious theological reflection in an academic context. His emphasis on the role of experience—in salvation and in his theology—draws out in a very dynamic way the pastoral dimension of theological reflection and the theological dimension of pastoral life. For DuBose, human experience and theological reflection are deeply related. They must not be divorced from each other. There is theological significance in what "rings true" to faith and helps people grow in faith (and what does not). Similarly, the fruits of theological reflection have much to say about how we present and share Christian faith. Pastoral life cut off from theological reflection can quickly become superficial. Theological reflection cut off from the realities of living the faith can quickly become abstract and unreal. DuBose connects theological reflection and the life of faith in a powerful way.

This relationship of pastoral and systematic concerns is revealed by the important role of the church in DuBose's theological system. In many respects, the church is the focal point for DuBose's theology. By the Spirit through the church we are outwardly and visibly included in the Incarnation. Through the church we may encounter the objective offer of salvation in Christ and participate in the subjective completion of the saving process in our lives. The church exists to make salvation available in our lived experience. We share in the saving process by our free participation in the life and sacraments of the church.

DuBose is concerned with the saving life of faith. He seeks to understand deeply the realities that he speculates about and describes. But his speculation is never just a mental exercise or an abstract activity. His concern is for salvation as a reality in our lives and in the church. DuBose seeks understanding so that faith may be deepened and shared more fully. His theology is not just *about* soteriology—it is *for our salvation.*

Accordingly, DuBose's theological reflections tend to culminate in his ecclesiology. It is in the church that the saving realities are to be known and lived. He thereby connects pastoral and systematic theological concerns in a very powerful way. Theological understanding adds depth to the life of faith, as the lived experience of faith shapes and animates theology. Indeed, our participation in the saving process may well include theological reflection on the way of life and love that saves us. Whatever the depth and complexity of DuBose's systematic theological analysis, his theology is always ultimately a pastoral theology of our salvation.

Furthermore, understanding DuBose's pneumatology is essential for comprehending his theological system. The activity of the Spirit is the unifying principle of DuBose's systematic theology of salvation because it is the

Spirit who makes the way of salvation possible for us. The Spirit prepares our hearts and wills for the saving process by which we subjectively realize the objective gift of salvation. The Spirit's mission in our lives is one of preparation, invitation, guidance, beckoning, and empowering for completion.

The dynamic role of pneumatology in DuBose's work points to the importance of *openness* in our individual lives and in the life of the church. Because of human free will, attitude is everything for our participation in the saving process. If we refuse to receive the Spirit's gift, salvation will not be forced upon us. The Spirit does not violate us or displace us in the name of salvation. We are not saved against our wills. Our salvation is to be a cooperative process by which we freely receive and give ourselves to God's saving love. By grace through faith, we are included in the Incarnation and share its saving benefits.

Our participation in the activity of the Spirit points to the fact that we are not self-sufficient. We cannot save ourselves, no matter how clever or strong we may be. We need a savior. We need Jesus, our savior, to be actively present by the Spirit in our lives and in the church. Our lack of self-sufficiency also underscores our need for openness. In and of ourselves, we do not have all we need for life. It is only as we receive and cooperate with God's loving gift of grace that we are saved. We must be open to the help from beyond ourselves that God lovingly offers. Jesus recognized his human limitations, and turned from self to God. We must do the same.

The ecumenical implication of this openness is that no single expression, faction or sect of the church has all truth. We need each other in the church. The fullness of spiritual truth is to be known and experienced in the church as a whole. Different groups and factions of religious people need each other for their mutual completion, because no group is complete in itself. Ecumenism is rooted in our need, not our tolerance. This provides significant guidance for ecumenical work. Our need calls for a spirit of openness within and among churches. We must participate in a process of listening that involves different perspectives and viewpoints. We may call this process the *open forum* of the church.

The unity we share in Christ is discovered as we allow our differences to "work themselves out." But our unity in Christ is the only basis for the church's open forum. The unity we share with others in Christ precedes all negotiations or overtures concerning our differences. No effort of our own—including our efforts to have an open forum—can be the ultimate basis for unity in Christ. Our unity in Christ, like the salvation it means, is a gift from God. The Spirit draws us together in the one body of Christ, which is the church.

The church is the unity we share with Christ and with each other in Christ's name. The unity we discover with one another saves us. We are to be at-one with God and one another in the life and sacraments of the church, thus sharing in Jesus' saving experience. Since it is our at-one-ment with Christ and with each other in Christ that saves us, and since it is preeminently in the church by the Spirit that we share unity in Christ, we should do all we can to make the church's unity outward and visible as well as inward and spiritual.

DuBose's pneumatology is significant for the praxis of Christian churches, entities, and organizations. If we believe in the present activity of the Spirit in our lives and our church, if we share DuBose's vibrant pneumatology, we can live the open forum. We can be open to a process of consensus-seeking and discernment at all levels of the church. This "listening together" in the midst of conflict and disagreements is as much needed in a parish vestry or board meeting as in an international ecumenical dialogue between denominations.

Despite our diversities and disagreements, we can listen together and receive help from beyond ourselves by the Spirit. We can be unafraid to allow consensus to emerge. We can compare our tentative conclusions with the revelations of God's activity we have already received through Scripture and tradition. We can know that the gift of salvation in Christ through the Incarnation is a continuing process, continuing to unfold in our world through the Spirit. This unfolding may take place in ways we had not imagined. We must be open enough to place no limits on God. We must be open to receive God's love for our salvation wherever it may be found.

This openness is particularly important in the ecumenical dialogues of Christian churches. We can affirm the truth and saving reality we find in other churches without betraying loyalty to our own tradition. We can discover the unity in Christ that we already share. We can be secure enough in our own truth to listen with open minds and hearts to the truth as perceived by others with different perspectives. We can be sensitive to ways that our truth may correct and be corrected by the truth that others perceive. Despite our differences, we can "listen together" with other Christians for ways in which we may be united by the one truth of salvation in Christ.

With respect to the ecumenical orientation of DuBose's theology, it is interesting to note that many of his last published writings appeared in the ecumenical journal the *Constructive Quarterly*. In terms of modern scholar-

ship concerning DuBose, it is also interesting to note that the two anthologies of his work published in the 1980s were edited respectively by a
Lutheran and a Roman Catholic.[9] DuBose's work continues to have ecumenical significance and interest today.

Finally, we may see that DuBose's emphasis on the living reality of salvation suggests a helpful guide for discernment and evaluation concerning
any doctrine, teaching, or practice of the church. DuBose's soteriology suggests one question as the criterion for discernment and evaluation: *Does it
serve the purpose of salvation?*

For example, with respect to the liturgy, we may ask whether a particular practice enhances and encourages the participation of the people, or
if it relegates them to the role of passive spectators. A liturgy that invites
participation may encourage a more active engagement in the life and sacraments of the church. And that more active engagement can serve the purpose of salvation. Such liturgical participation can help people experience
God's love in themselves and in others gathered to be the body of Christ in
the world. This can certainly encourage the subjective actualizing of faith.

On the other hand, a liturgical practice that causes people to feel dis-
tanced and removed from the life of the church, or unworthy and unwel-
come to participate in the church, would seem *not* to serve the purpose of
salvation. Whatever the depth and complexity of a teaching, whatever the
mystery and beauty of a symbol or devotion, whatever the seeming importance of a practice or tradition—it must ultimately be evaluated as it serves
the purpose of salvation. If we may experience or recall or be deepened in
the saving process through *anything*, we have a good reason to continue it.
And if *anything* obscures or distracts us from the saving process, we have a
good reason to avoid it. In making these judgments, it is important to recall
that although DuBose clearly upholds the importance of individual experience, he gives particular emphasis to the experience of the church as a
whole. In light of personal experience and especially the corporate experience of the church, we ask, "What serves the purpose of salvation?" These
are important lessons from DuBose's soteriology for the church and for
Christians.

DuBose urges that salvation is available through the life and sacraments of the church. His emphasis on experience is unwavering. Through
the church we may encounter, recall, and experience the reality of salvation.
The teaching, worship, and practices of the church make salvation-in-
Christ *available* to our experience. The life and sacraments of the church
will then signify and *be* most effectively what they are to signify and be—our

salvation in Christ through the Holy Spirit, our way for the completing of the saving process of Christ's Incarnation, our means for personal realization of God's love by grace through faith.

DuBose presents a theology of personally experienced salvation that is to be a living reality for us. Christ is made present for our salvation and we can share the saving process of the Incarnation by the Spirit through the church. By the Spirit, the objective gift of salvation in Christ is made available to us in our lives and in the church. The Spirit likewise enables our subjective participation and receiving of salvation, so that the objective truth of salvation in Christ becomes an increasing reality in us. As we freely cooperate with the saving process, the truth of salvation in Christ will be increasingly realized in our lives. When salvation in Christ is completed, our very being will be the fulfilment of God's life in us and our life in God, in whom we live and move and have our being.

Notes

CHAPTER 1

1. William Porcher DuBose, *The Reason of Life* (New York: Longmans, Green & Co., 1911), 30.

2. W. H. Moberly, "The Theology of Dr. DuBose," *Journal of Theological Studies* 9 (January 1908): 161; John Spence Johnston, review of *Turning Points in My Life, Church Quarterly Review* (October 1912): 71; Charles Winters, review of *A DuBose Reader, Saint Luke's Journal of Theology* 29, no. 1 (December 1985): 61. Winters notes that Armentrout's *Reader* provides "the framework of a book on systematic theology, with a chapter on each of the cardinal loci such a book should contain." See Donald S. Armentrout, ed., *A DuBose Reader: Selections from the Writings of William Porcher DuBose* (Sewanee, Tenn.: University of the South, 1984).

3. William Porcher DuBose, "Reminiscences," 10. Unpublished autobiographical reflections compiled by William Haskell DuBose, 1946. Manuscript. School of Theology Library, University of the South, Sewanee, Tenn.

4. Theodore DuBose Bratton, *An Apostle of Reality: The Life and Thought of the Reverend William Porcher DuBose* (London: Longmans, Green & Co., 1936), 3–8.

5. Ibid., 5.

6. William Porcher DuBose, *Turning Points in My Life* (New York: Longmans, Green & Co., 1912), 37–38. Thirty-five years after his capture, DuBose had a friendly reunion with Cronin, the Union soldier who captured him. DuBose had helped Cronin, "a faithful and deserving old soldier from Pennsylvania," prove his entitlement to a veteran's pension. DuBose recalled that Cronin said of their encounter at Boonesboro Gap, "I had come near killing him, and he had come nearer killing me."

7. Ibid., 39.

8. Charles Reagan Wilson, *Baptized in Blood: The Religion of the Lost Cause, 1865–1920* (Athens: University of Georgia Press, 1980), 148; Arthur Benjamin Chitty, Jr., *Reconstruction at Sewanee: The Founding of the University of the South and Its First Administration, 1857–1872* (Sewanee, Tenn.: University Press, 1954), 142 n. 1.

9. "Reminiscences," 141; Armentrout, "William Porcher DuBose: An Introduction to the Man," xvii. About 100 years later, DuBose was twice honored by St. John's, Winnsboro. In June 1962, the parish house chapel was named the William Porcher DuBose Chapel, and on September 18, 1966, a DuBose memorial stained glass window was dedicated in the parish church. Sharon Goff Avery, *History of Saint John's Episcopal Church, Winnsboro, South Carolina, 1839–1989* (Spartanburg, S.C.: Reprint Company, 1995), 204, 211, 213.

10. Ibid., 151.

11. Bratton, *An Apostle of Reality*, 78.

12. Armentrout, "William Porcher DuBose: An Introduction to the Man," viii–xx.

13. Donald Smith Armentrout, *The Quest for the Informed Priest* (Sewanee, Tenn.: School of Theology, University of the South, 1979), 121.

14. Armentrout, "William Porcher DuBose: An Introduction to the Man," xxi–xxii.

15. Review of *High Priesthood and Sacrifice*, *Church of Ireland Gazette*, July 31, 1908.

16. "The Theology of DuBose," review of *DuBose As a Prophet of Unity*, *Church Times* (London), February 13, 1925.

17. Ralph Luker, *A Southern Tradition in Theology and Social Criticism, 1830–1930: The Religious Liberalism and Social Conservatism of James Warley Miles, William Porcher DuBose and Edgar Gardner Murphy* [Studies in American Religion, Volume 11] (New York: Edwin Mellen Press, 1984), 228.

18. William Porcher DuBose to Silas McBee, March 7, 1908. McBee Papers, University of the South, Sewanee. Cited in Luker, *A Southern Tradition in Theology and Social Criticism, 1830–1930*, 255 n. 61.

19. Silas McBee to William Porcher DuBose, February 29, 1912. McBee Papers, Sewanee. Cited in Luker, *A Southern Tradition in Theology and Social Criticism, 1830–1930*, 401 n. 40.

20. "The Faith of a Christian Today," in *Unity in the Faith*, ed. W. Norman Pittenger (Greenwich, Conn.: Seabury Press, 1957), 206–18 (206 n. 1).

21. Luker, *A Southern Tradition in Theology and Social Criticism, 1830–1930*, 402.

22. William Porcher DuBose, "A Constructive Treatment of Christianity," in *Unity in the Faith*, ed. Pittenger, 35–36.

23. Cited in Luker, *A Southern Tradition in Theology and Social Criticism, 1830–1930*, 414.

24. "Dr. DuBose and His Students," *Churchman*, August 19, 1911: 255.

25. *Turning Points*, 15.

26. Armentrout, *The Quest for the Informed Priest*, 111. He takes the same position in an introduction to *A DuBose Reader*, in which he refers to DuBose's "six major writings." Armentrout, "DuBose's Theology: An Introduction to the Work," in *A DuBose Reader*, xxv. He refers to DuBose's "six major books" in an article on DuBose for the *Saint Luke's Journal of Theology*. Donald S. Armentrout, "William Porcher

DuBose and the Quest for the Informed Priest," *Saint Luke's Journal of Theology* 31, no. 4 (September 1988): 258–61.

27. Don S. Armentrout, review of *William Porcher DuBose: Selected Writings*, *Saint Luke's Journal of Theology* 32, no. 4 (September 1989): 295. Armentrout also takes the position that *Turning Points* was "autobiographical and personal" and not a "major book" in a signed entry on DuBose for the *Dictionary of Christianity in America*. D. S. Armentrout, "DuBose, William Porcher (1836–1918)," *Dictionary of Christianity in America*, ed. Daniel G. Reid (Downers Grove, Ill.: InterVarsity Press, 1990), 367. Armentrout's position is shared by other church historians. David L. Holmes also takes the position that DuBose "published six theological works." David L. Holmes, *A Brief History of the Episcopal Church* (Valley Forge, Pa.: Trinity Press International, 1993), 123. Luker refers to DuBose's "half-dozen theological works" in a signed entry on DuBose for the *Encyclopedia of Religion in the South*. Ralph E. Luker, "DuBose, William Porcher (1836–1918)," *Encyclopedia of Religion in the South*, ed. Samuel S. Hill (Macon, Ga.: Mercer University Press, 1984), 211.

28. Armentrout, *The Quest for the Informed Priest*, 112.

29. J. O. F. Murray, *Du Bose As a Prophet of Unity* (London: Society for Promoting Christian Knowledge, 1924), 23 (lecture 1), 46 (lecture 3). (A series of lectures of the DuBose Foundation, delivered at the University of the South.) Murray was the master of Selwyn College, Cambridge. This book was based on his lectures to the students of theology for the DuBose Memorial Foundation on November 7–10, 1922, at the University of the South, Sewanee, Tennessee. This was the inaugural series of lectures of the DuBose Foundation.

30. Murray, *Du Bose As a Prophet of Unity*, 5 (emphasis added).

31. "Reminiscences," 134.

32. *Turning Points*, 48–50.

33. Albert Sidney Thomas, *A Historical Account of the Protestant Episcopal Church in South Carolina, 1820–1957, Being a Continuation of Dalcho's Account, 1670–1820* (Columbia, S.C.: R. L. Bryan Company, 1957), 625.

34. "Reminiscences," 139–46; *Turning Points*, 39.

35. "Reminiscences," 154.

36. *Turning Points*, 87.

37. "Transfiguration Sermon," in *Turning Points*, 120–21.

38. *Turning Points*, 118.

39. Ibid., 110. This address was read by DuBose at a Sunday school conference that took place at Sewanee on the day after the DuBose Reunion. Ibid., 12.

40. Ibid., 18–19.

41. "Evangelical and Catholic: Each Needs the Other, Both Need the Church, and the Church Needs Both," in *Unity in the Faith*, 188–205, 199.

42. "Reminiscences," 30.

43. *Turning Points*, 21.

44. Ibid., 22.

45. "Reminiscences," 30.

46. *Turning Points*, 17.

47. Ibid., 21.

48. Ibid., 22–23.

49. Ibid., 23.

50. Ibid., 23–24.

51. "The Theology of the Child," in *Turning Points*, 98.

52. *Turning Points*, 20.

53. "Liberty and Authority in Christian Truth," in *Turning Points*, 131.

54. "Reminiscences," 37.

55. Ibid., 27–28.

56. Ibid., 69–70.

57. *Turning Points*, 30. Princeton Seminary was founded in New Jersey in 1812. Archibald Alexander (1772–1851) was elected the first professor at the seminary, where he "set the new center of conservative divinity on its course" (Sydney E. Ahlstrom, *A Religious History of the American People* [New Haven: Yale University Press, 1972], 462). Alexander brought to Princeton Seminary "not only scholarly attainments and an interest in rigid doctrinal orthodoxy but also a warmly pietistic religion, reflecting his own personal religious experience" ("Alexander, Archibald," in *The Westminster Dictionary of Church History*, ed. Jerald C. Brauer [Philadelphia: Westminster Press, 1971], 18). Charles Hodge (1797–1878) was the most noted professor at Princeton Seminary, where he taught from 1820 to 1878. Hodge authored a three-volume *Systematic Theology* (1872–1873). Princeton theology presented a conservative "American variant of Calvinism." It was based on Scottish common-sense rationalism, and it emphasized the verbal inerrancy of Scripture. This was understood to counter the "undermining" of faith in the authority of the Bible by biblical criticism (Brauer, ed., "Princeton Theology," in *The Westminster Dictionary of Church History*, 674). Hodge bragged that during his long tenure at the seminary, "not one new idea crept into or originated at Princeton." The Princeton theology later "became transformed into the more intellectual forms of fundamentalism" (Martin E. Marty, *Pilgrims in Their Own Land: 500 Years of Religion in America* [New York: Penguin Books, 1985], 303).

58. *Turning Points*, 30–32. The five points of Calvinism, formulated at the Synod of Dort (1618), were the total depravity of humanity, unconditional election, limited atonement, irresistible grace, and the perseverance of the saints.

59. Ibid., 31–32.

60. Ibid., 30–31.

61. Ibid., 31–32.

62. Ibid., 7–8.

63. Ibid., 5.

64. Bratton, *An Apostle of Reality*, 93.

65. *Turning Points*, 4–8.

66. Bratton, *An Apostle of Reality*, 90.

67. *Turning Points*, 8.

68. "Evangelical and Catholic," in *Unity in the Faith*, 189. In this context he seems to mean the Episcopal Church or the Anglican Communion when he speaks of "the Church," as distinguished from "the wider field of Christianity."

69. "Evangelical and Catholic," in *Unity in the Faith,* 189–205.

70. *Turning Points,* 7.

71. Ibid., 80.

72. "The Theology of the Child," in *Turning Points,* 111. This was DuBose's conclusion to his address on "The Theology of the Child" at the Sunday school conference.

73. George Townshend, "The DuBose Reunion: An Impression," *Churchman* (August 19, 1911): 265.

74. William Porcher DuBose, *The Gospel in the Gospels* (New York: Longmans, Green & Co., 1906), 207.

75. *Reason of Life,* 5–6.

76. William Porcher DuBose, *The Gospel According to Saint Paul* (New York: Longmans, Green & Co., 1907), 240.

77. "Christian Defense," in *Unity in the Faith,* 219–43.

78. *Turning Points,* 44.

79. *Gospel in the Gospels,* 280–81.

80. *Turning Points,* 42.

81. William Porcher DuBose, *The Ecumenical Councils,* vol. 3 of *Ten Epochs of Church History,* ed. John Fulton (New York: Christian Literature Company, 1896), 33.

82. *Gospel According to Saint Paul,* 285.

83. *Ecumenical Councils,* 34–35.

84. *Reason of Life,* 204.

85. William Porcher DuBose, *High Priesthood and Sacrifice: An Exposition of the Epistle to the Hebrews* (New York: Longmans, Green & Co., 1908), 111–12.

86. *Ecumenical Councils,* 44.

87. Ibid., 320.

88. *Reason of Life,* 77.

89. "Constructive Treatment of Christianity," in *Unity in the Faith,* 35–51.

90. *Turning Points,* 19–20. DuBose quotes John 3:8, from Jesus' explanation to Nicodemus about being born anew of the Spirit.

91. Ibid., 20. See Augustine, *Confessions,* trans. R. S. Pine-Coffin (Harmondsworth, England: Penguin Books, 1961), 21 (I, 1).

92. *Reason of Life,* 114, 118, 165, 120–30.

CHAPTER 2

1. William Porcher DuBose, *The Soteriology of the New Testament* (New York: Macmillan Company, 1892), 8.

2. Ibid., 298.

3. *High Priesthood and Sacrifice,* 220.

4. *Soteriology,* 195.

5. Ibid., 289.

6. Ibid., 290.

7. Ibid., 290.

8. *Gospel in the Gospels*, 141, 202.

9. Ibid., 232.

10. *Reason of Life*, 274.

11. "Resurrection," in *Unity in the Faith*, 85.

12. *Gospel in the Gospels*, 184.

13. *High Priesthood and Sacrifice*, 106–7.

14. *Soteriology*, 278.

15. Ibid., 336, 332–33.

16. Ibid., 333.

17. Ibid., 336.

18. Ibid., 218 (emphasis added).

19. Ibid., 27 (emphasis added).

20. Ibid., 55 (emphasis added).

21. Ibid., 4 (emphasis added).

22. *High Priesthood and Sacrifice*, 112 (emphasis added).

23. *Soteriology*, 32–33.

24. *Reason of Life*, 271, 270.

25. "Christian Defense," in *Unity in the Faith*, 241.

26. *Gospel According to Saint Paul*, 233.

27. *Ecumenical Councils*, 30. DuBose makes this statement relative to Peter's "famous confession of the person of the Lord" (Matthew 16:16–17).

28. *High Priesthood and Sacrifice*, 157.

29. *Soteriology*, 167.

30. *Reason of Life*, 258.

31. *Gospel According to Saint Paul*, 250, 253.

32. *High Priesthood and Sacrifice*, 208.

33. "Christian Defense," in *Unity in the Faith*, 239.

34. *Soteriology*, 84.

35. Ibid., 87.

36. *Gospel According to Saint Paul*, 253–54.

37. *Reason of Life*, 272. For the parable of the Pharisee and the publican, see Luke 18:9–14.

38. *Soteriology*, 200.

39. Ibid., 85.

40. *Gospel According to Saint Paul*, 7.

41. *High Priesthood and Sacrifice*, 156.

42. *Gospel According to Saint Paul*, 5.

43. *High Priesthood and Sacrifice*, 149, 142.

44. *Soteriology*, 193.

45. Ibid., 88. DuBose paraphrases Hebrews 2:8–9 in this quotation.

46. Ibid., 28.

47. *Gospel According to Saint Paul*, 284, 73–74.

48. *Gospel in the Gospels*, 153.

49. *Gospel According to Saint Paul*, 284.

50. *Soteriology*, 84.

51. B. B. Warfield, review of *The Gospel in the Gospels*, *Princeton Theological Review* 5 (October 1907): 690–97, 692.

52. *Gospel in the Gospels*, 176.

53. *Soteriology*, 365.

54. See Robert W. Prichard, *A History of the Episcopal Church* (Harrisburg, Pa.: Morehouse Publishing, 1991), 120; See also James Thayer Addison, *The Episcopal Church in the United States, 1789–1931* (New York: Charles Scribner's Sons, 1951), 211.

55. *Soteriology*, 59–60.

56. Ibid., 90.

57. *Gospel According to Saint Paul*, 277.

58. *Soteriology*, 167.

59. *Gospel in the Gospels*, 92–93, 149–50.

60. Ibid., 235.

61. *Reason of Life*, 174–75.

62. *Soteriology*, 121. DuBose makes this statement relative to Romans 6:7 and 1 Peter 4:1.

63. *High Priesthood and Sacrifice*, 212.

64. Ibid., 189, 176.

65. *Reason of Life*, 180. In this context DuBose comments (without citation) on 1 John 5:5–6, which refers to Jesus as "he that came by water and blood." *Reason of Life*, 179.

66. *Reason of Life*, 89.

67. *High Priesthood and Sacrifice*, 189, 14.

68. Ibid., 69, 22.

69. Ibid., 19, 22, 27.

70. *Gospel in the Gospels*, 151, 168.

71. *Gospel According to Saint Paul*, 233.

72. *Reason of Life*, 262.

73. Ibid., 262.

74. "Resurrection," in *Unity in the Faith*, 96.

75. Alister McGrath, *Justification by Faith: What It Means for Us Today* (Grand Rapids, Mich.: Zondervan, Academie Books, 1988), 52.

76. *Reason of Life*, 272.

77. Ibid., 272.

78. *Gospel According to Saint Paul*, 115.

79. *High Priesthood and Sacrifice*, 219.

80. Ibid., 218.

81. *Gospel According to Saint Paul*, 244.

82. *Soteriology*, 282.

83. *High Priesthood and Sacrifice*, 38, 21, 107.

84. *Gospel According to Saint Paul*, 52.

85. *High Priesthood and Sacrifice*, 49.

86. *Gospel According to Saint Paul*, 70.

87. *Soteriology*, 62–63, 350.

88. *Gospel According to Saint Paul*, 182.

89. *Turning Points*, 19.

90. *Gospel According to Saint Paul*, 281.

91. *Reason of Life*, 29–30.

92. *Soteriology*, 70.

93. *Reason of Life*, 204.

94. *High Priesthood and Sacrifice*, 210.

95. *Reason of Life*, 271. For the parable of the Pharisee and the publican, see Luke 18:9–14.

96. *Gospel in the Gospels*, 73. For the parable of the prodigal or lost son, see Luke 15:11–32.

97. *Reason of Life*, 270.

98. Ibid., 268, 274.

99. *Gospel According to Saint Paul*, 194.

100. "Resurrection," in *Unity in the Faith*, 89.

101. *Gospel According to Saint Paul*, 104, 194–95.

102. *The Reason of Life*, 175–76. The context for this statement by DuBose is his consideration of 1 John 2:1–2, which he correlates with 2 Corinthians 5:19 and Romans 5:11.

103. Ibid., 273–74.

104. *Soteriology*, 333–34.

105. Ibid., 334. DuBose paraphrases Galatians 2:20.

106. *High Priesthood and Sacrifice*, 14, 40, 76.

107. *Soteriology*, 70.

108. *Ecumenical Councils*, 190.

109. *Soteriology*, 335–36, 126–27.

110. Ibid., 295.

111. *Gospel in the Gospels*, 68.

112. *Soteriology*, 43.

113. Ibid., 13.

114. *Reason of Life*, 99.

115. Ibid., 119, 121, 99.

116. *Turning Points*, 6–7.

117. John S. Marshall, "Editor's Preface," in *Reason and Freedom: Aristotle's Ethics of the Perfect Life/William Porcher DuBose*, ed. John S. Marshall (Sewanee, Tenn., 1955), n.p. This work is a paraphrased and edited version of DuBose's lectures on Aristotle's *Ethics*.

118. *Soteriology*, 7.

119. See *High Priesthood and Sacrifice*, 153, 195, 248.

120. *Gospel in the Gospels*, 25.

121. "Christ the Solution of Human Life," in *Unity in the Faith*, 118.

122. *Reason of Life*, 66.

123. *Soteriology*, 9–10.

124. *Reason of Life*, 16.

125. "Resurrection," in *Unity in the Faith*, 88.

126. "A Constructive Treatment of Christianity," in *Unity in the Faith*, 39.

127. *Reason of Life*, 55.

128. Thomas Aquinas, *Summa Contra Gentiles, Book Three: Providence, Part I*, trans. Vernon J. Bourke (Notre Dame, Ind.: University of Notre Dame Press, 1975), 73 (3:17 [8]). See *Summa contra Gentiles, Book Three: Providence, Part I*, 74 (3:18[3]).

129. Ibid., 76 (3:19[1]).

130. Ibid., 97 (3:25[2]).

131. Ibid., 102 (3:25[14]).

132. Thomas Aquinas, *Summa Theologica*, trans. Fathers of the English Dominican Province, five volumes (Westminster, Md.: Christian Classics, 1981), 595 (pt. I-II, q. 2, art. 8).

133. Ibid., 602 (pt. I-II, q. 3, art. 8).

134. *High Priesthood and Sacrifice*, 62–63, 182–83.

135. *Gospel in the Gospels*, 222.

136. *Gospel According to Saint Paul*, 32, 26.

137. *Gospel in the Gospels*, 275.

138. *Soteriology*, 14, 26, 97.

139. Victor Lyle Dowdell, *Aristotle and Anglican Religious Thought* (Ithaca, N.Y.: Cornell University Press, 1942), 81. See W. H. Moberly, "The Theology of Dr. Du Bose," *Journal of Theological Studies* 9 (January 1908): 161–87, 177.

140. Dowdell, *Aristotle and Anglican Religious Thought*, 81.

141. David L. Holmes, *A Brief History of the Episcopal Church* (Valley Forge, Pa.: Trinity Press International, 1993), 124.

142. *Gospel in the Gospels*, 248–49, 225.

143. *Reason of Life*, 195.

144. *Soteriology*, 170.

145. *Gospel in the Gospels*, 48.

146. *Soteriology*, 171.

147. *Gospel According to Saint Paul*, 262.

148. *Soteriology*, 123.

149. "Christian Defense," in *Unity in the Faith*, 243.

150. *Reason of Life*, 53, 21, 41–42.

151. *Ecumenical Councils*, 84.

152. Pierre Teilhard de Chardin, *Science and Christ*, trans. René Hague (New York: Harper & Row, 1968).

153. *Reason of Life*, 26.

154. Jan A. Aertsen, "Aquinas' Philosophy in Its Historical Setting," in *The Cambridge Companion to Aquinas*, ed. Norman Kretzmann and Eleonore Stump (Cambridge: Cambridge University Press, 1993), 12–37 (16). Aquinas uses this interpreta-

tive scheme in his commentary on the *Sentences* of Peter Lombard (d. 1160). Aertsen explains that Aquinas's "scheme of exitus and reditus is derived from Neoplatonism and plays a fundamental role in Aquinas' thought. The origin and end of things are one and the same. The dynamics of reality is a circular motion (circulatio)."

155. *Reason of Life*, 28.

156. Ibid., 30.

157. Ibid., 27.

158. Ibid., 13.

159. Ibid., 105–6.

160. "Christian Defense," in *Unity in the Faith*, 236.

161. *Reason of Life*, 44.

162. *Soteriology*, 339.

163. *Ecumenical Councils*, 84.

164. *High Priesthood and Sacrifice*, 163–64.

165. "A Constructive Treatment of Christianity," in *Unity in the Faith*, 50.

166. *High Priesthood and Sacrifice*, 163.

167. *Soteriology*, 218.

168. *Gospel in the Gospels*, 137.

169. *Soteriology*, 27.

170. Ibid., 27.

171. Ibid., 102.

172. *High Priesthood and Sacrifice*, 143.

173. Norman Pittenger, *Alfred North Whitehead* (Richmond: John Knox Press, 1969), 48–49.

174. Ibid., 51.

175. *Gospel According to Saint Paul*, 173.

176. *Gospel in the Gospels*, 36–37. DuBose makes this statement relative to his quotation, without citation, of 1 Peter 1:7, "that the proof of your faith, more precious than gold that perisheth though it is proved by fire, might be found unto praise and glory and honour." *Gospel in the Gospels*, 37.

177. *Gospel According to Saint Paul*, 134–35.

178. *High Priesthood and Sacrifice*, 52.

179. Ibid., 246–47.

180. *Gospel in the Gospels*, 61–62.

181. *Gospel According to Saint Paul*, 211.

182. Ibid., 58–59.

CHAPTER 3

1. *High Priesthood and Sacrifice*, 42.

2. *Reason of Life*, 85.

3. Francis J. Hall, review of *The Gospel in the Gospels*, *Living Church* (March 24, 1906): 738–39.

4. "The Theology of Du Bose," review of *Du Bose As a Prophet of Unity*, by J. O. F. Murray, *Church Times*, February 13, 1925.

5. John Pearce, review of *William Porcher DuBose: Selected Writings*, ed. Jon Alexander, *Churchman* 103, no. 1 (1989): 85–86.

6. *Reason of Life*, 179.

7. *Gospel According to Saint Paul*, 48.

8. *Ecumenical Councils*, xii–xiii. DuBose does not mention specific authors or texts in this context.

9. Ibid., 15.

10. Ralph Luker, *A Southern Tradition in Theology and Social Criticism, 1830–1930*, 265–66. Luker cites Everhard Digges La Touche, *The Person of Christ in Modern Thought* (Boston: Pilgrim Press, 1912), 350 n. 2.

11. Luker, *A Southern Tradition in Theology and Social Criticism, 1830–1930*, 265.

12. *Ecumenical Councils*, 15.

13. *Gospel According to Saint Paul*, 301.

14. *Soteriology*, xi.

15. *Ecumenical Councils*, 323, 198.

16. Ibid., 197.

17. Ibid., 198.

18. Ibid., 197–99.

19. Ibid., 339–40.

20. *Gospel According to Saint Paul*, 228.

21. *Soteriology*, vii.

22. W. P. DuBose, "'Thou Art the Christ': Answers to the Great Questions from Religious Leaders of To-Day," *Sunday School Times*, November 2, 1912, 693 (lesson for November 17).

23. "Why the Church— in Christianity," in *Unity in the Faith*, 64.

24. *Gospel According to Saint Paul*, 32–35, 303.

25. *High Priesthood and Sacrifice*, 4–5, 206.

26. *Gospel According to Saint Paul*, 33.

27. *Reason of Life*, 241.

28. *Soteriology*, xi, 144–45.

29. Ibid., 231.

30. *Reason of Life*, 138.

31. "Christ the Revelation of God," in *Unity in the Faith*, 145–46.

32. *Gospel According to Saint Paul*, 287.

33. *Soteriology*, 142.

34. *High Priesthood and Sacrifice*, 185.

35. *Gospel According to Saint Paul*, 37, 227. DuBose refers to John 5:30.

36. *High Priesthood and Sacrifice*, 101, 148, 185.

37. *Soteriology*, 231–32.

38. *Reason of Life*, 52.

39. See *Soteriology*, 231.

40. *Gospel in the Gospels,* 187.

41. Ibid., 6.

42. Ibid., 236.

43. Ibid., 139, 204.

44. *Gospel in the Gospels,* 261.

45. *Gospel According to Saint Paul,* 294–95.

46. *Gospel in the Gospels,* 216.

47. *High Priesthood and Sacrifice,* 246.

48. *Gospel in the Gospels,* 6, 216.

49. Arthur Michael Ramsey, *An Era in Anglican Theology, from Gore to Temple: The Development of Anglican Theology between* Lux Mundi *and the Second World War, 1889–1939* (New York: Charles Scribner's Sons, 1960), 31. (The Hale Memorial Lectures of Seabury-Western Theological Seminary, 1959.)

50. Langford, *In Search of Foundations: English Theology, 1900–1920* (Nashville: Abingdon Press, 1969), 203 n. 27. This declaration was signed by G. Body, H. R. Bramley, W. Bright, T. T. Carter, W. M. G. Ducat, C. W. Furse, D. Grieg, C. D. Hammond, W. H. Hutchins, J. O. Johnson, E. C. Lowe, and P. G. Medd.

51. Ramsey, *An Era in Anglican Theology, from Gore to Temple,* 33.

52. *Soteriology,* 235.

53. *Reason of Life,* 266.

54. *Ecumenical Councils,* 333, 338.

55. *Soteriology,* 235.

56. *Ecumenical Councils,* 332.

57. "The Faith of a Christian Today," in *Unity in the Faith,* 217–18.

58. *High Priesthood and Sacrifice,* 164.

59. *Soteriology,* 235.

60. Ibid., 187.

61. *Gospel According to Saint Paul,* 11.

62. *Soteriology,* 187.

63. Ibid., 232.

64. Jaroslav Pelikan, *The Emergence of the Catholic Tradition (100–600),* vol. 1 of *The Christian Tradition: A History of the Development of Doctrine* (Chicago: University of Chicago Press, 1971), 206.

65. *Gospel in the Gospels,* 268–69, 284.

66. Ibid., 273.

67. *High Priesthood and Sacrifice,* 238.

68. *Ecumenical Councils,* 335–36.

69. *Reason of Life,* 85.

70. *Ecumenical Councils,* 87–88, 339.

71. For example, the Gospel of Luke (2:39) records that the child Jesus "grew and became strong, filled with wisdom" (NRSV). DuBose notes that Jesus increased in physical stature, and experienced spiritual and moral human growth during his life on earth. Jesus grew in grace and faith, learning obedience by all the experiences of his natural life. *Soteriology,* 194.

72. *Soteriology*, 201.
73. *Gospel in the Gospels*, 76.
74. *Soteriology*, 142.
75. Ibid., 143.
76. *Ecumenical Councils*, 194.
77. *Soteriology*, 146–47.
78. *Gospel According to Saint Paul*, 300.
79. *High Priesthood and Sacrifice*, 187.
80. *Soteriology*, 150–51.
81. Ibid., 154.
82. *Reason of Life*, 86.
83. *Soteriology*, 215.
84. "Resurrection," in *Unity in the Faith*, 93.
85. *High Priesthood and Sacrifice*, 79.
86. *Soteriology*, 215.
87. "Resurrection," in *Unity in the Faith*, 92, 93. In this context DuBose recalls Jesus' statement, "Of myself I can do nothing." DuBose paraphrases John 5:30. See also John 5:19.
88. "Christ the Revelation of God," in *Unity in the Faith*, 146.
89. *Soteriology*, 155.
90. *Gospel According to Saint Paul*, 230. DuBose draws on Genesis 3:15.
91. *Gospel in the Gospels*, 157.
92. *Soteriology*, 224.
93. *Ecumenical Councils*, 184.
94. *Soteriology*, 197.
95. John Stewart Lawton, *Conflict in Christology: A Study of British and American Christology, from 1889–1914* (London: Society for Promoting Christian Knowledge, 1947), 282.
96. *Soteriology*, 151–52, 197, 199.
97. *Ecumenical Councils*, 261–62.
98. Ibid., 261.
99. Ibid., 261.
100. *Gospel in the Gospels*, 279–80.
101. *Reason of Life*, 55.
102. *Gospel in the Gospels*, 234.
103. *Reason of Life*, 249.
104. *High Priesthood and Sacrifice*, 40.
105. *Ecumenical Councils*, 330.
106. "The Subjective and Objective in Religion," in *Unity in the Faith*, 165.
107. *Gospel According to Saint Paul*, 280.
108. *Soteriology*, 35.
109. *Reason of Life*, 92–93.
110. *Soteriology*, 155.
111. *Gospel in the Gospels*, 264–65.

112. Ibid., 282.
113. Ibid., 282.
114. Ibid., 46, 156.
115. Ibid., 267–68.
116. *Gospel According to Saint Paul*, 281.
117. *Reason of Life*, 85.
118 . *High Priesthood and Sacrifice*, 238–39.
119. *Soteriology*, 103–4.
120. *Reason of Life*, 72.
121. *Soteriology*, 339.
122. *High Priesthood and Sacrifice*, 14.
123. *Soteriology*, 104–5.
124. *Gospel in the Gospels*, 87–88.
125. Ibid., 88.
126. *Ecumenical Councils*, 38, 341.
127. "Christian Defense," in *Unity in the Faith*, 239.
128. *Soteriology*, 105.
129. *High Priesthood and Sacrifice*, 104.
130. *Soteriology*, 292–93.
131. *Ecumenical Councils*, 332. DuBose refers to John 14:9.
132. *Gospel According to Saint Paul*, 270–71.
133. *Gospel in the Gospels*, 119–24.
134. "Christ the Solution of Human Life," in *Unity in the Faith*, 131.
135. Ibid., 130.
136. *Ecumenical Councils*, 340–41.
137. *Gospel in the Gospels*, 223, 59–60, 270, 89.
138. *Gospel According to Saint Paul*, 136. DuBose draws on Romans 5:3.
139. *High Priesthood and Sacrifice*, 231.
140. *Gospel in the Gospels*, 271.
141. *Ecumenical Councils*, 85.
142. *Gospel in the Gospels*, 271.
143. Ibid., 127.
144. *Ecumenical Councils*, 84–85.
145. *Soteriology*, 149, 155, 302.
146. *Gospel According to Saint Paul*, 84.
147. *Gospel in the Gospels*, 278.
148. *High Priesthood and Sacrifice*, 15, 6, 154.
149. *Soteriology*, 182.
150. "Christian Defense," in *Unity in the Faith*, 235.
151. *High Priesthood and Sacrifice*, 180.
152. *Gospel in the Gospels*, 241.
153. *Soteriology*, 341.
154. Ibid., 310.
155. Ibid., 55.

156. *Gospel According to Saint Paul*, 173–74, 107, 128.

157. *High Priesthood and Sacrifice*, 15.

158. *Soteriology*, 329.

159. Ibid., 55, 336–37.

160. "A Constructive Treatment of Christianity," in *Unity in the Faith*, 49.

161. *Reason of Life*, 190.

162. *Soteriology*, 243.

163. *Gospel in the Gospels*, 118.

164. *Soteriology*, 299.

165. Ibid., 171.

166. *High Priesthood and Sacrifice*, 77, 103–4, 47–48.

167. *Gospel According to St. Paul*, 144.

168. *Soteriology*, 303.

169. *Gospel in the Gospels*, 165.

170. *Soteriology*, 280.

171. Ibid., 104.

172. *Reason of Life*, 274.

173. *Soteriology*, 280, 301.

174. *Gospel According to Saint Paul*, 6. DuBose draws on Mark 10:38, and possibly Luke 12:50 and John 18:11, with respect to Jesus' cup and baptism.

175. *Soteriology*, 231–32, 301–2.

176. *Gospel in the Gospels*, 218–19.

177. Ibid., 203.

178. Ibid., 78

179. D. S. Cairns, *The Faith That Rebels: A Re-examination of the Miracles of Jesus* (London: Student Christian Movement Press, 1928), 33.

180. *Gospel in the Gospels*, 82–83.

181. Ibid., 78, 200, 81.

182. Ibid., 79, 200.

183. Ibid., 78–79, 218–19.

184. Ibid., 203–4.

185. Ibid., 205.

186. Ibid., 79.

CHAPTER 4

1. *Soteriology*, 56, 213, 59.

2. R. C. Moberly, *Atonement and Personality* (New York: Longmans, Green & Co., 1905), 167–68. The "remarkable coincidence" between the theological systems of DuBose and R. C. Moberly was frequently discussed by William Sanday. See Sanday, "Dr. W. P. DuBose," *Churchman* (December 7, 1918): 667–69. See also Sanday, *The Life of Christ in Recent Research* (New York: Oxford University Press, 1908), 266–78, 285–312; Sanday, *Christology and Personality* (New York:

Oxford University Press, 1911), 127–31. In "Dr. W. P. Du Bose," Sanday characterizes "the two systems" of Moberly and DuBose as "original and independent," and "yet fundamentally the same" (667). Sanday knew both Moberly and DuBose. Sanday notes that Moberly had read one of DuBose's books, and DuBose was "acquainted" with Moberly's writing. Nevertheless, Sanday was "convinced" that "in neither case" did their familiarity with each other "at all impair the originality of the development" of their respective theological systems (*The Life of Christ in Recent Research*, 267.)

3. *Reason of Life*, 207, 71, 156.

4. *Soteriology*, 177.

5. Ibid., 179–80.

6. *Gospel in the Gospels*, 280.

7. R. C. Moberly, *Atonement and Personality*, 168–69.

8. *Soteriology*, 178.

9. *Gospel in the Gospels*, 287–88.

10. Ibid., 186, 243–44.

11. *Soteriology*, 178.

12. *Ecumenical Councils*, 31.

13. *Soteriology*, 212.

14. *Gospel in the Gospels*, 47.

15. *Soteriology*, 241–42.

16. *High Priesthood and Sacrifice*, 239.

17. *Reason of Life*, 186.

18. *Soteriology*, 215, 197, 188.

19. Ibid., 143, 207.

20. Ibid., 26.

21. *Gospel in the Gospels*, 246.

22. *Soteriology*, 211.

23. Ibid., 356.

24. *Reason of Life*, 156.

25. *Soteriology*, 356, 213.

26. *Gospel in the Gospels*, 286.

27. Ibid., 281.

28. *High Priesthood and Sacrifice*, 239.

29. *Reason of Life*, 70. DuBose does not restrict the term "grace" to the activity of the Spirit. He notes that grace is also used in the New Testament (1) "to express an eternal and essential disposition of God"; (2) as the "special function" of the Word of God, "through Whom are mediated all God's operations in creation"; and (3) as "always in the World," coming into the world "in an eminent degree in the person of Jesus Christ."

30. *Gospel in the Gospels*, 81.

31. *Soteriology*, 342, 85.

32. Ibid., 164.

33. *High Priesthood and Sacrifice*, 58–59.

34. *Soteriology*, 83, 209.

35. *Gospel in the Gospels*, 245.

36. *High Priesthood and Sacrifice*, 60.

37. "Incarnation," in *Unity in the Faith*, 74.

38. *Soteriology*, 167.

39. Ibid., 207, 121.

40. *Reason of Life*, 149, 49.

41. "The Faith of a Christian Today," in *Unity in the Faith*, 212–13.

42. *Ecumenical Councils*, 42.

43. *Soteriology*, 378.

44. Ibid., 358, 362.

45. Ibid., 379. In this regard, DuBose recalls Jesus' inability to work miracles among the people in his own hometown: "He could not, because of their unbelief" (Matthew 13:58.)

46. Ibid., 384.

47. *Gospel in the Gospels*, 244.

CHAPTER 5

1. "The Church," in *Unity in the Faith*, 101.

2. "The Demand for the Simple Gospel," in *Unity in the Faith*, 181.

3. *Reason of Life*, 127–28.

4. "The Demand for the Simple Gospel," in *Unity in the Faith*, 181.

5. "A Constructive Treatment of Christianity," in *Unity in the Faith*, 50.

6. "The Church," in *Unity in the Faith*, 99.

7. *Soteriology*, 379, 213.

8. "The Church," in *Unity in the Faith*, 110.

9. *Soteriology*, 252, 379.

10. "Why the Church—in Christianity," in *Unity in the Faith*, 58–59.

11. *Soteriology*, 379.

12. Ibid., 389.

13. *Gospel According to Saint Paul*, 181.

14. *Soteriology*, 382.

15. Ibid., 382–83.

16. Ibid., 383, 369–70.

17. Ibid., 383.

18. "Evangelical and Catholic," in *Unity in the Faith*, 204.

19. *Soteriology*, 370.

20. Ibid., 344–45.

21. Ibid., 383.

22. Ibid., 364.

23. Ibid., 364.

24. Ibid., 367.

25. Ibid., 367.

26. *Soteriology,* 351–52.

27. *Gospel According to Saint Paul,* 251–52.

28. *Soteriology,* 367.

29. Ibid., 362, 358, 344.

30. Ibid., 43.

31. Ibid., 44.

32. *Gospel in the Gospels,* 179.

33. Ibid., 179.

34. *Soteriology,* 125.

35. Ibid., 125.

36. *High Priesthood and Sacrifice,* 207.

37. *Soteriology,* 42.

38. Ibid., 252.

39. Ibid., 361.

40. Ibid., 361.

41. *Gospel in the Gospels,* 243.

42. *High Priesthood and Sacrifice,* 219.

43. *Gospel According to Saint Paul,* 180, 178.

44. *Soteriology,* 117. DuBose makes this point in commenting on St. Paul's statement in 1 Corinthians 11:26 "that 'as often as (in the Eucharist) we eat the bread and drink the cup we do set forth the Lord's death until He come.'" Ibid., 116.

45. Ibid., 348.

46. Ibid., 351. DuBose quotes Romans 6:4 in this context: "We were buried with Him by baptism into death that as Christ was raised from the dead by the glory of the Father, so we also should walk in newness of life."

47. *Gospel According to St. Paul,* 180, 181.

48. "Why the Church—in Christianity," in *Unity in the Faith,* 59–60.

49. *Soteriology,* 371.

50. Ibid., 351.

51. *High Priesthood and Sacrifice,* 219.

52. *Soteriology,* 371.

53. "Evangelical and Catholic," in *Unity in the Faith,* 203.

54. *Soteriology,* 366.

55. Ibid., 366–67.

56. "The Subjective and Objective in Religion," in *Unity in the Faith,* 172.

57. *Soteriology,* 360.

58. Ibid., 361.

59. Ibid., 375.

60. *Ecumenical Councils,* 43.

61. Ibid., 37–38.

62. Ibid., 46–47.

63. Ibid., 46.

64. Ibid., 46.

65. Ibid., 43.

66. "William Porcher DuBose," *The Proper for the Lesser Feasts and Fasts, 1994*, 330.

67. *Ecumenical Councils*, 43.

68. Ibid., 321.

69. Ibid., 28.

70. Ibid., 233–34. Cyril of Alexandria (d. 444) led the third General Council to depose Nestorius (d. c. 451) and condemn his teaching. Nestorianism acknowledged two persons (divine and human) in Christ, and rejected the term "Theotokos."

71. Ibid., 28.

72. Ibid., 203–4.

73. Ibid., 321.

74. *Gospel in the Gospels*, 4.

75. *Turning Points*, 121.

76. Robert B. Slocum, "Discovering the Truth, William Porcher DuBose Sought a 'Living' Approach to Theology," *Living Church*, August 16, 1992: 9. See Robert B. Slocum, "Living the Truth: An Introduction to the Theological Method and Witness of William Porcher DuBose," *Saint Luke's Journal of Theology* 34, no. 1 (December 1990): 28–40, 32.

77. "Liberty and Authority in Christian Truth," in *Turning Points*, 140.

78. Ibid., 143, 140–41.

79. Ibid., 131–32.

80. Ibid., 127.

81. *Gospel According to Saint Paul*, 13.

82. *Gospel in the Gospels*, x–xi.

83. *Ecumenical Councils*, 29, 321.

84. Murray, *Du Bose As a Prophet of Unity*, 43.

85. Ibid., 43.

86. *Gospel According to Saint Paul*, 3.

87. Ibid., 3.

88. *Reason of Life*, 10–11.

89. *Turning Points*, 12. See "The Theology of the Child," in *Turning Points*, 95–111.

90. W. P. DuBose, "Letter to the Rt. Rev. C. M. Beckwith (June 26, 1899)," in *The Trinity Course of Church Instruction: A Method of Teaching the Book of Common Prayer in the Sunday-Schools of the Church*, comp. C. M. Beckwith (New York: Edwin S. Gorham, 1903), 4–5. See also DuBose, "'Thou Art the Christ': Answers to the Great Question from Religious Leaders of To-Day," 693. DuBose was among "a large number of leading scholars in North America and Great Britain" who published a brief "expression of their personal belief in the deity of our Lord" in the *Sunday School Times*.

91. *Gospel According to Saint Paul*, 12, 13.

92. W. P. DuBose, preface to *Liberal and Mystical Writings of William Law* (New York: Longmans, Green & Co., 1908), vii–xviii, viii.

93. "Liberty and Authority in Christian Truth," in *Turning Points*, 135–36, 138. This article was originally published in the December 8, 1906, issue of the *Churchman*, and reprinted in the March 22, 1924, issue of the *Churchman*. According to an editorial note accompanying "Liberty and Authority in Christian Truth" in the March 22, 1924, issue, this article by DuBose was originally published "soon after the conviction of Dr. Crapsey for heresy." See W. P. DuBose, "Liberty and Authority in Christian Truth," *Churchman* (March 22, 1924): 10–12 (10 [editorial note]). The Rev. Algernon Sidney Crapsey, rector of St. Andrew's Church, Rochester, New York, was convicted of heresy in the Diocese of Western New York in 1906. He was convicted of impugning the divinity, conception by the Holy Spirit, virgin birth, and resurrection of Jesus; impugning the doctrine of the Trinity; and denying the conception by the Holy Spirit, virgin birth, and resurrection of Jesus. He was also convicted of breaking his ordination vows to conform to the doctrine, discipline, and worship of the Episcopal Church, and to "drive away from the Church all erroneous and strange doctrines contrary to God's Word." See "Decision of the Court," *Journal of the Seventieth Annual Council of the Protestant Episcopal Church in the Diocese of Western New York* (1907), 95–99.

94. "Christian Defense," in *Unity in the Faith*, 226.

95. *High Priesthood and Sacrifice*, 3.

96. Ibid., 3.

97. Ibid., 4.

98. "Liberty and Authority in Christian Truth," in *Turning Points*, 143.

99. Ibid., 143.

100. *Gospel According to Saint Paul*, 14.

101. *Gospel in the Gospels*, 128.

102. *Gospel According to Saint Paul*, 157.

103. *Ecumenical Councils*, 36.

104. Ibid., xii.

105. *Reason of Life*, 1.

106. Ibid., 1–2.

107. "Liberty and Authority in Christian Truth," in *Unity in the Faith*, 128.

108. *Reason of Life*, 9–10.

109. "Preparedness: Some Essential Preliminaries to Christian Unity," *Churchman* (February 13, 1932): 10–12. This essay by DuBose began as a supportive response to a "Call to Preparedness for the task of religious reconstruction," proposed as a "Formula of Comprehension and Reconciliation." The "Formula of Comprehension" was proposed by the Rev. Gardiner L. Tucker, field secretary of the Board of Religious Education in the Province of Sewanee (southeastern United States) of the Episcopal Church. It states that the Episcopal Church "has in her official terminology two words, 'Catholic' and 'Protestant' which are not contradictory but complementary, each of which stands for a necessary side of the fulness of Christian Truth and Life" (quoted p. 10).

110. "Liberty and Authority in Christian Truth," in *Turning Points*, 129.

111. "Preparedness: Some Essential Preliminaries to Christian Unity, Part II," 13.

112. *Reason of Life*, 10.

113. Ibid., 10.

114. "The Church," in *Unity in the Faith*, 111.

115. *Reason of Life*, 9.

116. "The Church," in *Unity in the Faith*, 111–12.

117. Ibid., 100, 111.

118. *Reason of Life*, 10–11.

119. "Liberty and Authority in Christian Truth," in *Unity in the Faith*, 127.

120. "Evangelical and Catholic," in *Unity in the Faith*, 188, 205.

121. "Constructive Treatment of Christianity," in *Unity in the Faith*, 36–37.

122. "The Church," in *Unity in the Faith*, 115.

123. "Constructive Treatment of Christianity," in *Unity in the Faith*, 37.

124. Ibid., 37. DuBose does not identify any specific Christian sects in this context.

125. "Constructive Treatment of Christianity," in *Unity in the Faith*, 37.

126. "The Church," in *Unity in the Faith*, 112.

CHAPTER 6

1. *Soteriology*, 213.

2. *Reason of Life*, 78.

3. "Christ the Solution of Human Life," in *Unity in the Faith*, 138.

4. *Reason of Life*, 100.

5. Ibid., 172.

6. Ibid., 231–34.

7. Ibid., 248.

8. Ibid., 222.

9. Armentrout is a pastor of the Evangelical Lutheran Church of America. He is professor of church history and associate dean for academic affairs at the School of Theology, the University of the South, where DuBose taught. Alexander is a Roman Catholic and a member of the Dominican Order.

Bibliography

THE WRITINGS OF WILLIAM PORCHER DUBOSE

Books

The Ecumenical Councils. Vol. 3 of *Ten Epochs of Church History.* Edited by John Fulton. New York: Christian Literature Company, 1896. (A second edition of *The Ecumenical Councils* was published by T. & T. Clark of Edinburgh.)

The Gospel According to Saint Paul. New York: Longmans, Green & Co., 1907.

The Gospel in the Gospels. New York: Longmans, Green & Co., 1906. (Many reprintings until 1923).

High Priesthood and Sacrifice: An Exposition of the Epistle to the Hebrews. New York: Longmans, Green & Co., 1908. (The Bishop Paddock Lectures at the General Theological Seminary, New York, 1907–1908).

The Reason of Life. New York: Longmans, Green & Co., 1911.

The Soteriology of the New Testament. New York: Macmillan Company, 1892. (New edition, with a new preface, 1899).

Turning Points in My Life. New York: Longmans, Green & Co., 1912. (Including "The Theology of the Child," "Sermon Preached in the University Chapel, Sewanee, on the Feast of the Transfiguration, 1911," and "Liberty and Authority in Christian Truth.")

Unity in the Faith. Edited by W. Norman Pittenger. Greenwich, Conn.: Seabury Press, 1957. (Eleven essays originally published in the *Constructive Quarterly*; and the article "Christian Defense," originally published in the *Sunday School Teacher's Manual.* These essays and articles are listed separately below.)

Articles, Essays, and Sermons

"Address at Fairmont School, Monteagle, Tennessee." Undated manuscript. University Archive, University of the South.

"Address." In *Semi-Centennial of the University of the South, 1857–1907: Sermon, Poem, Addresses and Letters,* 83–90. Sewanee, Tenn.: University Press, 1907.

"Adventures of an Adjutant." *Weekly News* (Charleston, S.C.), October 4, 1882.

The Christian Ministry: A Sermon Preached at the Ordination of Rev. O. T. Porcher, Abbeville, S.C., May 15th, 1870. Charleston: Walker, Evans & Cogswell, 1870.

"Christ the Revelation of God." *Constructive Quarterly* 5, no. 4 (December 1917): 655–70.

"Christ the Solution of Human Life." *Constructive Quarterly* 5, no. 2 (June 1917): 201–24.

"Christianity the World Religion: An Appreciation of the Bishop of Southwark's 'The Fullness of Christ.'" *Churchman* (May 29, 1909): 774–76.

"The Church." *Constructive Quarterly* 5, no. 1 (March 1917): 1–18.

"A Constructive Treatment of Christianity." *Constructive Quarterly* 1 (March 1913): 5–21.

"The Death of Sin." Sermon. Undated manuscript. University Archive, University of the South.

"The Demand for the Simple Gospel." *Constructive Quarterly* 6, no. 3 (September 1918): 417–31.

"Dr. John Bell Henneman." *Sewanee Review* 17, no. 1 (January 1909): 108–14.

"Edgar Gardner Murphy: An Appreciation." *Sewanee Review* 22, no. 4 (October 1914): 494–97.

"Ellison Capers." *Sewanee Review* 16, no. 3 (July 1908): 368–73.

"Evangelical and Catholic: Each Needs the Other, Both Need the Church, and the Church Needs Both." *Constructive Quarterly* 8, no. 3 (September 1920): 345–62.

"The Faith of a Christian Today: My Faith in the Presence of Doubts; Not Doubts That Have Arisen in My Faith." *Constructive Quarterly* 6, no. 4 (December 1918): 577–89.

"George Rainsford Fairbanks." *Sewanee Review* 14, no. 4 (October 1906): 498–503.

"Herbert Spencer's Data of Ethics." Undated manuscript. University Archives, University of the South.

"Incarnation." *Constructive Quarterly* 4, no. 3 (September 1916): 249–66.

"The Interpretation of the Bible in Relation to the Present Condition of Learning and Science." In *The Fifth Annual Church Congress,* 25–27. New York: M. H. Mallory & Co., 1878.

Introduction to *The Church and the Jew,* by Bernard Gruenstein, vi–vii. Sewanee, Tenn.: University Press at the University of the South, 1907.

"The Joint Commission on Marginal Readings." *Churchman* (March 4, 1899): 323.

"The Late Course of Religious Thought." In *Matthew Arnold and the Spirit of the Age: Papers of the English Club of Sewanee,* edited by Greenough White, 44–50. New York: G. P. Putnam's Sons, 1898.

"Letter to the Rt. Rev. C. M. Beckwith, July 26, 1899." In *The Trinity Course of Church Instruction: A Method of Teaching the Book of Common Prayer in the Sunday-Schools of the Church,* compiled by C. M. Beckwith, 4–5. New York: Edwin S. Gorham, 1903.

"Liberty and Authority in Christian Truth." *Churchman* (December 8, 1906): 902–4. Reprinted in the *Churchman* 129 (March 22, 1924): 10–12; and in *Turning Points,* 125–43.

"Permanence and Progress in the Interpretation of Christian Symbols." In *The Seventeenth Church Congress in the United States*, 125–31. New York: Thomas Whittaker, 1896.

Preface to *Liberal and Mystical Writings of William Law*, by William Scott Palmer, vii–xviii. New York: Longmans, Green & Co., 1908.

"Preparedness: Some Essential Preliminaries to Christian Unity." *Churchman* (February 13, 1932): 10–12; "Part II." *Churchman* (February 20, 1932): 13–15.

"The Professor in the University." *Churchman* (February 11, 1899): 210.

"Protestant-Catholic: Extracts from a Correspondence between the Rev. Wm. P. DuBose, S.T.D., and One of His Disciples." *St. Andrew's Cross* 43, no. 1 (October, 1928): 9–10.

"Recollections of Mt. Zion School." *Educational* (Columbia, S.C.) 1, 1 (February 1, 1902): 256–60.

"Resurrection." *Constructive Quarterly* 4, no. 4 (December 1916): 788–800.

"The Resurrection as a Practical Principle." *Churchman* (April 9, 1898): 527–28.

"The Romance and Genius of a University." *Sewanee Review* 13, no. 4 (October 1905): 496–502. Reprinted in the *Sewanee News* 32, no. 3 (August 1966): 10–11.

"The Sacramental Idea." In *The Church Congress Journal*, 211–18. New York: Thomas Whittaker, 1913.

"A Saint of the Southern Church." *Sewanee Review* 5, no. 4 (October 1897): 486–92. Greenough White, *Memoir of the Right Reverend Nicholas Hamner Cobbs, D.D., First Bishop of the Diocese of Alabama, with notices of some of his contemporaries. A contribution to the religious history of the Southern States.* New York: James Pott & Co., 1897.

"St. Paul and the Spiritual Interpretation of the Creeds." *Churchman* (December 1, 1906): 843–44.

"Sermon Preached in the University Chapel, August 6, 1911 [the DuBose Reunion at Sewanee.]" *Churchman* 104 (August 19, 1911): 263–64. Reprinted in *Turning Points*, 113–23. An excerpted version of this sermon appeared as "Sewanee Sermon," *Anglican Digest* 40, no. 4 (Transfiguration 1998): 46–47.

"Sermon Preached at a Meeting of St. Luke's Brotherhood, Sewanee, Tennessee." Undated manuscript. University Archives, University of the South.

"Sermon Preached at the Opening of All Saints Church, Sewanee, Tennessee, May 22, 1910." University Archives, University of the South Sewanee, Tenn.

"The Sincerity of the Christian Ministry." *Churchman* (February 2, 1901): 128–29. (Originally a sermon preached at the ordination of John Beean, Sewanee, Tenn., July 1900.)

"The Student and the University." *Churchman* (February 18, 1899): 248.

"The Subjective and Objective in Religion." *Constructive Quarterly* 6, no. 1 (March 1918): 39–56.

"The Teaching of Our Lord as to the Indissolubility of Marriage." *Forensic Quarterly* 1, no. 1 (November 1909): 63–64.

"The Theology of the Child." In *Turning Points*, 95–111. (An address read by

DuBose at a Sunday school conference that followed the August 1911 DuBose Reunion at Sewanee.)

"'Thou Art the Christ': Answers to the Great Questions from Religious Leaders of To-Day." *Sunday School Times*, November 2, 1912, 693 (lesson for November 17).

"Thoughts for Lent." *Churchman* (February 24, 1912): 258.

"Three Lost Arts." *Sewanee Review* 15, no. 2 (April 1907): 166–72.

"The University of the South." In William Stevens Perry, *The Organization and Progress of the American Church, 1783–1883*, 557–60. Vol. 2 of *The History of the American Episcopal Church 1587–1883*. Boston: James R. Osgood & Co., 1885.

"Wade Hampton." *Sewanee Review* 10, no. 3 (July, 1902): 364–68.

"The Word of God." Unpublished manuscript, marked "from Silas McBee Collection." University Archives, University of the South.

"The Word of God." In "The Church's Call to the Study of the Bible, Tuesday Morning, June 23." In *General Report with the Addresses at the Devotional Meetings*, 70–74. Vol. 1 of *Pan-Anglican Congress, 1908*. London: Society for Promoting Christian Knowledge, 1908.

"What Is Christianity? A Review of Harnack's Reply." *Churchman* 84 (October 26, 1901): 538–39. Adolf von Harnack, *What is Christianity? Lectures delivered in the University of Berlin during the winter-term 1899–1900*, trans. Thomas Bailey Saunders. New York: G. P. Putnam's; London: Williams and Norgate, 1901.

"What Is Faith?" *Sunday School Times*, May 29, 1909, 275.

"Why the Church—in Christianity." *Constructive Quarterly* 3, no. 2 (June 1915): 249–66.

Anthologies of or Including DuBose's Work

Documents of Witness: A History of the Episcopal Church, 1782–1985, 173–76, 407–18. Edited by Don S. Armentrout and Robert Boak Slocum. New York: Church Hymnal Corporation, 1994.

A DuBose Reader: Selections from the Writings of William Porcher DuBose. Compiled by Donald S. Armentrout. Sewanee, Tenn.: University of the South, 1984.

William Porcher DuBose, Selected Writings. Edited by Jon Alexander, O.P. Sources of American Spirituality. New York: Paulist Press, 1988.

Other Unpublished Manuscripts

"From Aristotle to Christ." Written by DuBose 1913–1918. Typewritten paper, edited by Alberry Charles Cannon, Jr., 1963. University Archives, University of the South. Based on DuBose's lectures at the University of the South on the *Ethics* of Aristotle.

"Reason and Freedom, Aristotle's Ethics of the Perfect Life." Edited by John S. Marshall, Sewanee, Tenn., 1955. An edited and rephrased version of "From Aristotle to Christ," available at the University of the South Library.

"Reminiscences." Autobiographical reflections, compiled by William Haskell
DuBose, 1946. School of Theology Library, University of the South.

WRITINGS ABOUT OR MENTIONING WILLIAM PORCHER DUBOSE

Books

Addison, James Thayer. *The Episcopal Church in the United States, 1789–1931.* New
York: Charles Scribner's Sons, 1951.

Ahlstrom, Sydney E. *A Religious History of the American People.* New Haven: Yale
University Press, 1972.

Albright, Raymond W. *A History of the Protestant Episcopal Church.* New York:
Macmillan, 1964.

Alexander, Jon, O.P. *American Personal Religious Accounts, 1600–1980.* New York:
Edwin Mellen Press, 1983.

Armentrout, Donald Smith. *The Quest for the Informed Priest.* Sewanee, Tenn.:
School of Theology, University of the South, 1979.

Avery, Sharon Goff. *History of Saint John's Episcopal Church, Winnsboro, South Carolina, 1839–1989.* Spartanburg, S.C.: Reprint Company, 1995.

Bratton, Theodore DuBose. *An Apostle of Reality: The Life and Thought of the Reverend
William Porcher DuBose.* New York: Longmans, Green & Co., 1936. (A series of
lectures of the DuBose Foundation delivered at the University of the South.)

Cave, Sydney. *The Doctrine of the Person of Christ.* London: Duckworth, 1925.

Cheshire, Joseph Blount. *The Church in the Confederate States: A History of the Protestant Episcopal Church in the Confederate States.* New York: Longmans, Green &
Co., 1912.

Chitty, Arthur Benjamin, Jr. *Reconstruction at Sewanee: The Founding of the University
of the South and its First Administration, 1857–1872.* Sewanee, Tenn.: University Press, 1954.

DeMille, George E. *The Episcopal Church Since 1900.* New York: Morehouse-Gore-
ham Co., 1955.

Denney, James. *The Christian Doctrine of Reconciliation.* New York: George H. Doran
Co., 1918. Cunningham Lectures for 1917.

Digges La Touche, Everhard. *The Person of Christ in Modern Thought.* Boston: Pilgrim Press, 1912.

Dowdell, Victor Lyle. *Aristotle and Anglican Religious Thought.* Ithaca, N.Y.: Cornell
University Press, 1942.

Fairbanks, George R. *History of the University of the South, at Sewanee, Tennessee: From
Its Founding by the Southern Bishops, Clergy and Laity of the Episcopal Church in
1857 to the Year 1905.* Jacksonville: H. & W. B. Drew Co., 1905.

Guerry, Moultrie, Arthur Ben Chitty, and Elizabeth N. Chitty. *Men Who Made
Sewanee.* Sewanee, Tenn.: University Press, 1981.

Hall, Francis J. *The Kenotic Theory, Considered with Particular Reference to Its Anglican
Forms and Arguments.* New York: Longmans, Green & Co., 1898.

Hendry, George S. *The Gospel of the Incarnation*. Philadelphia: Westminster Press, 1958.

Holmes, David L. *A Brief History of the Episcopal Church, with a Chapter on the Anglican Reformation and an Appendix on the Quest for an Annulment of Henry VIII*. Valley Forge, Pa.: Trinity Press International, 1993.

Holmes, Urban T., III. *What Is Anglicanism?* Wilton, Conn.: Morehouse-Barlow, 1982.

Hoskyns, Edwyn Clement. *The Fourth Gospel*, edited by Francis Noel Davey. London: Faber and Faber Limited, 1947.

Inge, W. R. *Faith and Its Psychology*. London: Duckworth, 1909.

Jones, Rufus M. *A Preface to Christian Faith in a New Age*. New York: Macmillan, 1932.

Lawton, John S. *Conflict in Christology: A Study of British and American Christology from 1889–1914*. London: Society for Promoting Christian Knowledge, 1947.

Luker, Ralph. *A Southern Tradition in Theology and Social Criticism, 1830– 1930: The Religious Liberalism and Social Conservatism of James Warley Miles, William Porcher DuBose and Edgar Gardner Murphy*. Vol. 11 of Studies in American Religion. New York: Edwin Mellen Press, 1984.

Mackintosh, H. R. *The Doctrine of the Person of Jesus Christ*. Edinburgh: T. & T. Clark, 1978.

Mackintosh, Robert. *Historic Theories of Atonement, with Comments*. London: Hodder and Stoughton, 1920.

Macquarrie, John. *Jesus Christ in Modern Thought*. Valley Forge, Pa.: Trinity Press International, 1990; London: SCM Press, 1990.

Marshall, John S., ed. *Reason and Freedom: Aristotle's Ethics of the Perfect Life/William Porcher DuBose*. Sewanee, Tenn., 1955. This work is a paraphrased and edited version of DuBose's lectures on Aristotle's *Ethics*.

———. *The Word Was Made Flesh: The Theology of William Porcher DuBose*. Sewanee, Tenn.: University Press, 1949.

McBee, Silas. *An Eirenic Itinerary: Impressions of Our Tour with Addresses and Papers on the Unity of Christian Churches*, 88. London: Longmans, Green, & Co., 1911.

Mozley, J. K. *The Doctrine of the Atonement*. New York: Charles Scribner's Sons, 1916.

———. *Some Tendencies in British Theology, from the Publication of* Lux Mundi *to the Present Day*. London: Society for Promoting Christian Knowledge, 1951.

Murray, J. O. F. *DuBose as a Prophet of Unity*. London: Society for Promoting Christian Knowledge, 1924. (A series of lectures of the DuBose Foundation delivered at the University of the South.)

Nichols, James Hastings. *Romanticism in American Theology: Nevin and Schaff at Mercersburg*. Chicago: University of Chicago Press, 1961.

Percy, Walker Alexander. *Lanterns on the Levee: Recollections of a Planter's Son*. New York: Alfred A. Knopf, 1941.

Pittenger, W. Norman. *The Word Incarnate: A Study of the Doctrine of the Person of Christ*. New York: Harper & Brothers, 1959.

Ramsey, Michael. *Holy Spirit: A Biblical Study*. Cambridge, Mass.: Cowley, 1992.

Sanday, William. *Christology and Personality*. New York: Oxford University Press, American Branch, 1911.

———. *The Life of Christ in Recent Research*. New York: Oxford University Press, 1908.

Shattuck, Gardiner H., Jr. *A Shield and Hiding Place: The Religious Life of the Civil War Armies*. Macon, Ga.: Mercer University Press, 1987.

Smith, James Ward, and A. Leland Jamison. *Religion in American Life*. Vol. 1 of *The Shaping of American Religion*, 298–303, 307 (Ahlstrom essay); 467–68 (Daniel D. Williams essay). Princeton: Princeton University Press, 1961.

Taylor, Vincent. *Jesus and His Sacrifice: A Study of the Passion-Sayings in the Gospels*. London: Macmillan & Co., 1955.

———. *The Person of Christ in New Testament Teaching*. London: Macmillan & Co., 1958.

Thomas, Albert Sidney. *A Historical Account of the Protestant Episcopal Church in South Carolina, 1820–1957, Being a Continuation of Dalcho's Account, 1670–1820*. Columbia, S.C.: R. L. Bryan Company, 1957.

Tucker, Louis. *Clerical Errors*. New York: Harper & Brothers, 1943.

von Hügel, Friedrich. *Letters from Baron Friedrich von Hügel to a Niece*, edited by Gwendolen Greene. Chicago: Henry Regnery Company, 1955.

Wilson, Charles Reagan. *Baptized in Blood: The Religion of the Lost Cause, 1865–1920*. Athens: University of Georgia Press, 1980.

Wilson, John M. *I Have Looked Death in the Face: Biography of William Porcher DuBose*. Kingston, Tenn.: Paint Rock Publishing, Inc., 1996.

Wilson, William E. *The Problem of the Cross: A Study of New Testament Teaching*. London: James Clarke & Co., Ltd., 1929.

Dissertations or Theses

Barker, Frederick Thomas. "Holiness, Righteousness, and Life: The Theology of William Porcher DuBose." Ph.D. diss., Drew University, 1985.

Foss, Charles Sanford. "In Current Coin: A Study of the Theology of William Porcher DuBose." Ph.D. diss., Graduate Theological Union, 1989.

Guerry, Moultrie. "A Study of the Process of Atonement according to William Porcher DuBose." B.D. thesis, Virginia Theological Seminary, 1925.

Kezar, Dennis Dean. "Many Sons to the Father's Glory: A Study of Salvation Theory in the Works of William Porcher DuBose." D.Phil. diss., New College, Oxford University, 1974.

Newberry, Charles Gomph. "The Christology of William Porcher DuBose." S.T.B. thesis, General Theological Seminary, 1954.

Ralston, William Henry, Jr. "William Porcher DuBose: A Study in the Methodology of Christian Apologetics." S.T.M. thesis, General Theological Seminary, 1956.

Slocum, Robert B. "Living the Truth: The Theological Method and Witness of William Porcher DuBose." D.Min. thesis, School of Theology, University of the South, 1992.

Williams, Theodore Martin. "Humanity and Logos: An Essay in the Theology of William Porcher DuBose." Ph.D. diss., Emory University, 1973.

———. "The Purpose of God: An Essay in the Theology of William Porcher DuBose." S.T.M. thesis, School of Theology, University of the South, 1971.

Articles and Essays

Ahlstrom, Sydney E. "Theology in America: A Historical Survey." In *The Shaping of American Religion,* edited by Smith and Jamison, 232–321 (298–303, 307).

Alexander, Jon, O.P. Introduction to *William Porcher DuBose: Selected Writings,* 3–51.

"Appreciation of Dr. William Porcher DuBose." *The Witness,* September 14, 1918: 3. Reprinted in *Sewanee Purple* 35, no. 1 (October 10, 1918): 2.

Armentrout, Donald S. "The Beginnings of Theological Education at the University of the South: The Role of John Austin Merrick." *Historical Magazine of the Protestant Episcopal Church* 51:3 (September 1982): 253–67 (264).

———. "DuBose's Theology: An Introduction to the Work." In *A DuBose Reader,* edited by Armentrout, xxv–xxxix.

———. "William Porcher DuBose: An Introduction to the Man." In *A DuBose Reader,* edited by Donald S. Armentrout, xiii–xxiv.

———. "William Porcher DuBose and the Quest for the Informed Priest." *Saint Luke's Journal of Theology* 31, no. 4 (September 1988): 255–74.

Bailey, Thomas P. "The Angelical Doctor of Sewanee." *Sewanee Review* 26, no. 4 (October 1918): 493–96.

Bayne, Stephen. "'In the Mine, Not in the Mint': A Sketch of the Life of William Porcher DuBose." *St. Luke's Journal of Theology* 15 (Summer 1972): 3–18. (Paper read at the 1970 DuBose Symposium, Charleston, S.C.)

Bremond, H. "Letter to the DuBose Reunion." *Churchman* (August 19, 1911): 266.

Cannon, Alberry Charles. "Editor's Preface: From Aristotle to Christ." Summer 1971. Unpublished manuscript. University Archives, University of the South.

Carus, Paul. "William Porcher Du Bose: A Christian Philosopher." *Monist* 20, no. 1 (January 1910): 144–53.

Chitty, Arthur Ben. "Heir of Hopes: Historical Summary of the University of the South." *Historical Magazine of the Protestant Episcopal Church* 23, no. 2 (September 1954): 258–65 (258).

Chitty, Elizabeth N. "DuBose Reunion [Sewanee Now and Then]." *Sewanee Mountain Messenger,* November 3, 1989, 3.

Compton, Stephen C. "Edgar Gardner Murphy and the Child Labor Movement." *Historical Magazine of the Protestant Episcopal Church* 52, no. 2 (June 1983): 181–94 (187–88).

"The Conferences and the Symposia [the DuBose Reunion at Sewanee]." *Churchman* (August 19, 1911): 265.

"Death of Dr. DuBose." *Living Church,* August 24, 1918: 555.

"Dr. DuBose." *Churchman,* August 31, 1918: 234.

"Dr. DuBose." *Palm Branch,* September 1918: 1.

"Dr. DuBose and His Students." *Churchman*, August 19, 1911: 255.

"Dr. DuBose and Modern Philosophic Thought." *Churchman*, August 19, 1911: 255–56.

"Dr. DuBose on the Principle of Unity." *Churchman*, November 25, 1911: 751.

"The DuBose Reunion at Sewanee." *Churchman*, August 12, 1911: 227.

"The DuBose Reunion at Sewanee." *Southern Churchman*, August 26, 1911: 10–11.

"DuBose Symposium Is Part of Tricentennial." *Savannah Morning News*, December 5, 1970, 7A.

Edwards, Dan. "Deification and the Anglican Doctrine of Human Nature: A Reassessment of the Historical Significance of William Porcher DuBose." *Anglican and Episcopal History* 58, no. 2 (June 1989): 196–212.

Essex, E. C. "The Atonement in Post-Reformation Writers." In *The Atonement in History and in Life: A Volume of Essays*, edited by L. W. Grensted (246–47). New York: Macmillan, 1929.

Fuller, Reginald H. Foreword to *A DuBose Reader*, edited by Donald S. Armentrout, ix.

Grant, Frederick C. "The Outlook for Theology." *Anglican Theological Review* 10, no. 1 (July 1927): 1–10 (8).

Gresham, J. Wilmer. "The Spirit of the Du Bose Reunion." *Living Church*, August 19, 1911: 543–44.

Guerry, Moultrie. "Makers of Sewanee: William Porcher Du Bose." *Sewanee Review* 41, no. 4 (October–December, 1933): 483–94.

Guerry, William Alexander. "William Porcher DuBose." *Churchman*, August 31, 1918: 237–38.

Guthrie, William Norman. "The Doctor, As I Knew Him." *Churchman*, December 15, 1936: 16–17.

Knickerbocker, William S. "Asides and Soliloquies." Review of *An Apostle of Reality*, by Theodore DuBose Bratton. *Sewanee Review* 45, no. 1 (January–March, 1937): 1–9.

Lanier, John J. "The South's Religious Thinkers." *Southern Literary Messenger* (January 1940): 19–24.

"The Late Dr. Du Bose." *Southern Churchman*, August 31, 1918: 1.

Luker, Ralph. "The Crucible of Civil War and Reconstruction in the Experiences of William Porcher DuBose." *South Carolina Historical Magazine* 83, no. 1 (January 1982): 50–71.

———. "Liberal Theology and Social Conservatism: A Southern Tradition, 1840–1920." *Church History* 50, no. 2 (June 1981): 193–204.

———. "William Porcher DuBose and a Southern Theological Tradition, 1840–1920." In *Varieties of Southern Religious Experience*, edited by Samuel S. Hill, 158–71.

MacDowell, Dorothy K. "Fairfield County." *South Carolina Magazine*, April, 1970: 16–23 (18–23).

Manning, William T. "An Apostle of Reality: The Life and Thought of William Porcher DuBose." Review of *An Apostle of Reality*, by Theodore DuBose Bratton. *Living Church* (October 24, 1936): 457–60, 463.

————. Introduction to *The Word Was Made Flesh*, by John S. Marshall, v–vii. Sewanee, Tenn.: University Press, 1949.

Macquarrie, John. "William Porcher DuBose and Modern Thought." *Saint Luke's Journal of Theology* 31, no. 1 (December 1987): 15–24.

————. "William Porcher DuBose: New Testament Scholar and Systematic Theologian." *Anglican Theological Review*, supplementary series 11 (March 1990): 140–53.

Marshall, John S. "From Aristotle to Christ; or, The Philosophy of William Porcher DuBose." *Sewanee Review* 51, no. 1 (January–March 1943): 148–59.

————. "Philosophy through Exegesis." *Anglican Theological Review* 26, no. 4 (October 1944): 204–12.

Martin, Franklin B. "Distinguished Alumnus." *Magazine of The Citadel* (Autumn 1957): 5:18.

McBee, Silas. "William Porcher DuBose: Address at the Unveiling of a Monument to His Memory at Sewanee, June 14th, 1920." *Constructive Quarterly* 8, no. 3 (September 1920): 507–28.

McCrady, Edward. Foreword to *Unity in the Faith*, edited by W. Norman Pittenger, v–viii.

Moberly, W. H. "The Theology of Dr. Du Bose." *Journal of Theological Studies* 9 (January 1908): 161–87.

Montgomery, H. H. "Letter to the DuBose Reunion." *Churchman*, August 19, 1911: 266.

Murray, J. O. F. "DuBose and the Problems of To-Day." *Constructive Quarterly* 9, no. 4 (December 1921): 537–57.

————. "DuBose as a Prophet of Unity: A Series of Lectures on the DuBose Foundation Delivered at the University of the South: Introduction and Lecture 1: The Background of Spiritual Experience." *Living Church*, February 17, 1923: 552–54.

————. "DuBose as a Prophet of Unity: Lecture 2: His Message and Its Foundation: Confidence in Truth." *Living Church*, February 24, 1923: 583–84.

————. "DuBose as a Prophet of Unity: Lecture 3: His Method—Spiritual Psychology." *Living Church*, March 3, 1923: 619–20.

————. "DuBose as a Prophet of Unity: Lecture 4: Human Need and the Origin of Sin." *Living Church*, March 10, 1923: 661– 62.

————. "DuBose as a Prophet of Unity: Lecture 5–I: DuBose's Doctrine of the Incarnation." *Living Church*, March 17, 1923: 693–94.

————. "DuBose as a Prophet of Unity: Lecture 5–II: DuBose's Doctrine of the Incarnation." *Living Church*, March 24, 1923: 733–34.

————. "DuBose as a Prophet of Unity: Lecture 6: Divine Self Limitation." *Living Church*, March 31, 1923: 772.

————. "DuBose as a Prophet of Unity: Lecture 7: The Logos as God Immanent in Creation." *Living Church*, April 7, 1923: 808–9.

————. "DuBose as a Prophet of Unity: Lecture 8: His Vision of God and of the Church." *Living Church*, April 14, 1923: 847–48.

————. "Letter to the DuBose Reunion." *Churchman*, August 19, 1911: 266.

Myers, George Boggan. "The Sage and Seer of Sewanee." In *Unity in the Faith*, edited by W. Norman Pittenger, 1–20.

Nevius, Richard C. "William Porcher DuBose and the Bible." Manuscript. University Archive, University of the South, Sewanee, Tenn. (Paper read at the 1970 DuBose Symposium in Charleston, S.C.)

Norris, R. A., Jr. "DuBose's Christology." Manuscript. University Archive, University of the South, Sewanee, Tenn. (Paper read at the 1970 DuBose Symposium in Charleston, S.C.)

——. "A Memorial for W. N. Pittenger." *Anglican Theological Review* 80:1 (Winter 1998): 3–7 (6).

Pittenger, W. Norman. Preface to *Unity in the Faith*, edited by W. Norman Pittenger, ix–xi.

——. "The Role of the Theologian." *Saint Luke's Journal of Theology* 1, no. 1 (St. Luke's Day 1957): 5–12. (Concerning DuBose's "significance in the theological world.")

Ribbing, Seved. "William Porcher DuBose—en lefnadsteckning." *God Jul!* (Stockholm) (December 15, 1909): 59–71. (English translation of this article available in the files of Donald S. Armentrout, School of Theology, University of the South.)

Sanday, William. "Dr. W. P. DuBose." *Churchman*, December 7, 1918: 667–69.

——. "Letter to the DuBose Reunion." *Churchman*, August 19, 1911: 266.

Shattuck, Gardiner H., Jr. "'The Work and Life of His Kingdom': Southern Episcopalians and the Lost Cause." In *This Sacred History, Anglican Reflections for John Booty*, ed. by Donald S. Armentrout (Cambridge, Mass.: Cowley Publications, 1990) 112–24, 120–21.

Slatterly, Charles Lewis. "The Reminiscences of Dr. DuBose." *Churchman*, May 25, 1912: 701.

Slocum, Robert B. "Christian Assurance in the Face of Death: Anglican Witnesses." *Sewanee Theological Review* 38, no. 2 (Easter 1995): 126–36.

——. "Discovering the Truth: William Porcher DuBose Sought a 'Living' Approach to Theology." *Living Church* (August 16, 1992): 9.

——. "The Lessons of Experience and the Theology of William Porcher DuBose." *Anglican Theological Review* 79, no. 3 (Summer 1997): 341–68.

——. "Living the Truth: An Introduction to the Theological Method and Witness of William Porcher DuBose." *Saint Luke's Journal of Theology* 34, no. 1 (December 1990): 28–40.

——. "Making-One with God: At-one-ment in the Theology of William Porcher DuBose." *Sewanee Theological Review* 35, no. 3 (Pentecost 1992): 264–73.

——. "Refiner's Fire: The Soteriology of Sacrifice in the Work of William Porcher DuBose." *Saint Luke's Journal of Theology* 34, no. 3 (June 1991): 41–47.

——. Review of *John Williamson Nevin, American Theologian*. *Anglican Theological Review* 80, no. 4 (Fall 1998): 615–16 (616).

———. "A Story to Tell: Personal Narrative in the Synthesis of Pastoral Experience and Theological Reflection." In *A New Conversation, Essays on the Future of Theology and the Episcopal Church*, ed. by Robert Boak Slocum (New York: Church Publishing, 1999). 20–35, 22–27, 31.

"The Theology of Du Bose." Review of *DuBose As a Prophet of Unity*, by J. O. F. Murray. *Church Times*, February 13, 1925.

Townshend, George. "The DuBose Reunion: An Impression." *Churchman*, August 19, 1911: 265.

"Who Was He—This Man Called William Porcher DuBose?" *Tennessee Churchman*, April 1977: 3. Reprinted in *Piedmont Churchman*, June 1977.

"William Porcher DuBose." *Churchman*, September 7, 1918: 261.

Winters, Charles L. "DuBose's Doctrine of the Church." Manuscript. University Archives, University of the South. (Paper read at the 1970 DuBose Symposium, Charleston, S.C.)

Woodruff, Ronald Lee. "DuBose's Doctrine of Salvation." Manuscript. University Archives, University of the South. (Paper read at the 1970 DuBose Symposium, Charleston, S.C.)

———. "A Theologian for Our Times." Review of *A DuBose Reader. Living Church*, February 17, 1985: 12–13.

Woolverton, John F. "Huntington's Quadrilateral: A Critical Study." *Church History* 39 (1970): 198–211 (204).

———. "John Williamson Nevin and the Episcopalians: The Debate on the 'Church Question,' 1851–1874." *Historical Magazine of the Protestant Episcopal Church* 49, no. 4 (December 1980): 361–87 (387).

Reviews of DuBose's Work

"Christianity the Universal Ministry of Life." Review of *The Reason of Life. Churchman* (February 17, 1912): 2.

"Dr. DuBose on the Principle of Unity." Review of *The Reason of Life. Churchman* 104 (November 25, 1911): 751.

Armentrout, Don S. *Review of William Porcher DuBose: Selected Writings, Saint Luke's Journal of Theology*, 32, no. 4 (September 1989): 295.

Dykes, J. Oswald. Review of *The Soteriology of the New Testament. Critical Review of Theological & Philosophical Literature* 3 (1893): 38–43.

Gailor, Thomas F. Review of *The Soteriology of the New Testament. Sewanee Review* 8 (April, 1900): 234–40.

Hall, Francis J. Review of *The Gospel in the Gospels. Living Church* (March 24, 1906): 738–39.

H. L. "Two Books on the Gospel." Review of *The Gospel in the Gospels* and *The Gospel According to St. Paul. Church Gazette* (December 1908): 275–76.

Hughes, John Jay. Review of *William Porcher DuBose, Selected Writings*, edited by Jon Alexander, O.P. *Theological Studies* 50, no. 2 (June 1989): 400.

Inge, W. R. Review of *The Reason of Life. Journal of Theological Studies* 13, no. 4 (January 1912): 316–17.

Johnson, John Spence. "Dr. DuBose and the University of the South." Review of *Turning Points. Church Quarterly Review* 75 (October 1912): 71–83.

Jones, Edward. Review of *A DuBose Reader: Selections from Writings of William Porcher DuBose*, edited by Donald S. Armentrout. *Encounter* 46 (Autumn 1985): 372–73.

Nash, Henry S. "Dr. DuBose's 'Gospel in the Gospels.'" *Sewanee Review* 15, no. 1 (January 1907): 111–20.

Pearce, John. Review of *William Porcher DuBose: Selected Writings*, edited by Jon Alexander, O.P. *Churchman* 103, no. 1 (1989): 85–86.

Ralston, William M. Review of *Unity in the Faith. Canadian Journal of Theology* 4 (July 1958): 234–36.

Review of *The Ecumenical Councils. Bibliotheca Sacra* 54 (January 1897): 197.

Review of *The Ecumenical Councils. Church Quarterly Review* 89 (October 1897): 246–48.

Review of *The Ecumenical Councils. Expository Times* 8, no. 11 (August 1897): 517.

Review of *The Ecumenical Councils. Guardian*, February 16, 1898.

Review of *The Gospel in the Gospels. Church Times*, August 3, 1906: 147–48.

Review of *The Gospel in the Gospels. Guardian*, July 4, 1906.

Review of *The Gospel in the Gospels. Spectator*, August 11, 1906: 204–5.

Review of *The Gospel According to St. Paul. Expository Times* 18 (August, 1907): 516.

Review of *High Priesthood and Sacrifice. Baptist Times*, August 6, 1908.

Review of *High Priesthood and Sacrifice. British Friend*, July 1908.

Review of *High Priesthood and Sacrifice. Christian World*, August 6, 1908.

Review of *High Priesthood and Sacrifice. Church of Ireland Gazette*, July 31, 1908: 657.

Review of *High Priesthood and Sacrifice. Church Quarterly Review* 67 (January 1909): 435–38.

Review of *High Priesthood and Sacrifice. Expository Times* 19 (August 1908): 518.

Review of *High Priesthood and Sacrifice. Scottish Standard Bearer* (September 1908).

Review of *High Priesthood and Sacrifice. Westminster Gazette* (August 22, 1908).

Review of *The Reason of Life. American Journal of Theology* 16, no. 2 (April 1912): 322–23.

Review of *The Reason of Life. Church Quarterly Review*, 74 (July 1912): 445–48.

Review of *The Reason of Life. Expository Times* 22 (December 1911): 100–101.

Review of *The Reason of Life. New York Times*, February 25, 1912, 105.

Review of *The Soteriology of the New Testament. Christian Union* (July 16, 1892).

Review of *The Soteriology of the New Testament. Church Eclectic* (March 1893): 1074–80.

Review of *The Soteriology of the New Testament. Churchman*, June 4, 1892: 729–30.

Review of *The Soteriology of the New Testament. Methodist Review* 74 (September 1892): 835.

Review of *The Soteriology of the New Testament. New York Tribune*, August 1, 1892.

Review of *The Soteriology of the New Testament. Public Ledger* (Philadelphia), June 24, 1892.

Review of *The Soteriology of the New Testament. Supplement to the Church of Ireland Gazette* (December 6, 1907): 1076–77.

Review of *Unity in the Faith*. *Holy Cross Magazine* 68, no. 11 (November 1957): 348.

Sanday, William. "The Gospel According to Saint Paul, First Part." *Churchman* (May 18, 1907): 717–20.

———. "The Gospel According to Saint Paul, Second Part." *Churchman* (May 25, 1907): 758–61.

———. "The Spiritual Meaning of the Life of Christ, First Part." Review of *The Gospel in the Gospels*. *Churchman* 93 (April 28, 1906): 644–45.

———. "The Spiritual Meaning of the Life of Christ, Second Part." Review of *The Gospel in the Gospels*. *Churchman* 93 (May 5, 1906): 679–82.

Slattery, Charles Lewis. "Dr. DuBose's 'Reason of Life.'" *Churchman* (February 17, 1912): 222.

Talbot, Edward S. "An Impression of Dr. DuBose's New Book." Review of *The Gospel in the Gospels*. *Churchman* (March 24, 1906): 447.

Tucker, Gardiner L. Review of *The Reason of Life*. *Sewanee Review* 20, no. 3 (July 1912): 391–92.

W. A. G. "A Sewanee Book Once More." Review of *The Ecumenical Councils*. *Sewanee Review* 6 (April 1898): 248–50.

Warfield, B. B. Review of *The Gospel in the Gospels*. *Princeton Theological Review* 5, no. 4 (October 1907): 690–97.

White, Greenough. "A Discussion of Historical Christology." Review of *The Ecumenical Councils*. *Sewanee Review* 5 (January 1897): 33–47.

Williams, Daniel D. "Tradition and Experience in American Theology." In *The Shaping of American Religion*, edited by Smith and Jamison, 443–95 (467–68).

Winters, Charles L. "Seabury Press Publishes William P. DuBose Book." Review of *Unity in the Faith*. *Sewanee Purple* 65, no. 26 (May 29, 1957): 1.

W. M. G. Review of *The Gospel in the Gospels*. *Church Standard* (November 3, 1906): 19–20.

W. R. S. Review of *The Reason of Life*. *Pax* (March 1912).

Index

miracles, 70ff.
mutuality (role of in salvation), 34–35,
    80, 91, 109f.

participation (in our own salvation),
    28–31, 89ff., 97, 109f., 112
pneumatology, 74ff., 107ff. 111ff.
poverty, 8
prodigal son, 26, 32, 33

Reason of Life, The, 28, 35, 98, 104
reconciliation, 89
regeneration, 27, 86f., 90
repentance, 31, 33
reunion (of DuBose's students), 5, 13,
    15
resurrection, 72
righteousness of Jesus, 59f., 71, 77f.

sacraments, 81f., 84ff., 90–92, 114

salvation, 20ff., 24ff., 107ff., 114
salvation, objective and subjective, 26f.,
    73, 75, 76, 80, 82, 86f., 89, 92
saving process, 24ff., 107f., 109
sin, 23, 31, 33, 42–44
sonship, 26, 31, 33, 42–44
soteriology, 20, 48, 108ff., 114
Soteriology of the New Testament, The, 20,
    48
Spirit, the, 74ff., 108ff., 111
Spirit Christology, 77ff.
suffering (role of in salvation), 64

teleology, 35ff.
truth, 92f., 96f., 99
Turning Points in My Life, 5, 6, 99

University of the South (Sewanee), 3

weakness of Jesus, 52ff.